THE SHELSLEY
WALSH STORY

SHELSLEY WALSH
HILL CLIMB

LENGTH OF COURSE : 1000 YARDS (914 M)
MINIMUM WIDTH : 12 FEET (3·66 M)
RISE IN HEIGHT : 328 FEET (100 M)
AVERAGE GRADIENT : 1:9·14
STEEPEST GRADIENT : 1:6·24

N

FINISH

MAIN STRAIGHT

Ⓐ

TOP 'S'

Ⓡ

BOTTOM 'S'

B/D

Ⓣ

MEMBERS TENT

⑤

COURT HOUSE

St ANDREW'S CHURCH

CROSSING

POND

Ⓐ

TO WORCESTER & MARTLEY

BAR

③

②

Ⓐ

B/D

Ⓣ

KENNEL BEND

PADDOCK

Ⓡ

①

START

Ⓐ

① THE OLD POST OFFICE

② THE LODGE

③ PADDOCK DUAL DRIVE

④ THE OLD RECTORY

⑤ FANE MEMORIAL SEAT

Ⓐ COMMENTATORS

Ⓡ REFRESHMENTS

Ⓣ TOILETS

B/D BREAKDOWN/INCIDENT VEHICLES

M.A.C OFFICE

CAR PARK

④

THE BARRACKS

TO STANFORD BRIDGE

R H 2001

THE SHELSLEY WALSH STORY

A century of motorsport

Simon Taylor

Foreword by Sir Stirling Moss

Haynes Publishing

DEDICATION

To my beloved Pearl, in gratitude for her endless patience

First published in April 2005

A catalogue record for this book is available from the British Library

ISBN 1 84425 090 3

Library of Congress catalog card no 2004 117160

Published by Haynes Publishing, Sparkford, Yeovil, Somerset BA22 7JJ, UK
Tel: 01963 442030 Fax: 01963 440001
Int.tel: +44 1963 442030 Int.fax: +44 1963 440001
E-mail: sales@haynes.co.uk
Website: www.haynes.co.uk

Haynes North America Inc., 861 Lawrence Drive, Newbury Park, California 91320, USA

Page-built and typeset by Christopher Fayers
Printed and bound in Britain by J. H. Haynes & Co. Ltd., Sparkford

CONTENTS

FOREWORD

by Sir Stirling Moss

I wish I could say I started my motorsport career at Shelsley Walsh. Well, I tried to! In 1948 I got a new Cooper 500 for my first season and proudly sent off my entry for the May Shelsley. To my dismay, it was returned. In those days, before circuit racing had got properly under way again after the war, Shelsley Walsh was just about the most important car event in the country. The meeting was over-subscribed and, not surprisingly, the organisers weren't going to chuck out a well-known name for some unknown teenager called S. Moss.

I tried again for the September meeting, and attached to my entry form a pleading letter, which I'm amused to find has survived in the Shelsley archives. I'd had a few wins by then, so I was accepted, and managed to win my class. I did both the 1949 Shelsleys too.

Then my life became so busy, racing for Jaguar and HWM around Europe, that I never managed to return. But I have always believed that Shelsley represented an important stage in my motor racing education. Hillclimbs are very unforgiving. Your run lasts only a few seconds, and the tiniest error or misjudgement will relegate you to the ranks of the also-rans. So it demands real discipline, focus and concentration, qualities which matter to a Grand Prix driver too.

That's why lots of top racing drivers went to Shelsley – before the war people like Raymond Mays, Rudi Caracciola, Whitney Straight and Hans Stuck and, in my own time, the likes of Peter Collins, Ken Wharton, Bob Gerard and Roy Salvadori. Today there are several rapid drivers,

Learning his craft: the teenage Stirling Moss hurls his 1100cc Cooper-JAP twin through the Esses in June 1949. His time of 38.57sec was an unsupercharged record.

September 1948, and the
teenage Stirling takes his
first 500cc Cooper out of
the Top Ess on his maiden
visit to Shelsley.

Moss prepares
for his June 1949 climb.
Father Alfred and
mother Aileen supervise,
mechanic Don Müller
is on the right.

Fifty years on, Sir Stirling returns from a demonstration climb in Terry Grainger's HWM-Jaguar – which Moss raced in 1950 in 2-litre guise.

like 2004 European Touring Car Champion Andy Priaulx, who started in hillclimbing and moved to circuit racing. I wonder how long it will be before somebody gives young Adam Fleetwood, the current RAC Hillclimb Champion, a circuit test in something like an F3 car? He could surprise a lot of people who don't realise how good hillclimbing is for developing racing talent.

Having done my last hillclimb in 1949, it wasn't until some 50 years later that I went back to Shelsley Walsh, at the invitation of the Midland Automobile Club. By then, needless to say, all of motorsport – the circuits, the cars, the business – had changed out of all recognition from the days when I competed in the 1950s and early 1960s. But I was delighted to find that Shelsley Walsh had changed very little. The fastest cars were totally up-to-the-minute, of course, and had benefited from the technical and aerodynamic advances seen in Formula One. The hill record, which was around 37 seconds when I was competing, had come down almost unbelievably into the mid-20s. But the atmosphere was just as I remembered it. The hill itself hadn't changed, nor had the paddock or the layout of the place. And the old spirit of sporting competition was alive and well.

It was all very heart-warming.

So when the Midland Automobile Club asked me to be Patron of the Shelsley Trust, I was happy to accept. The MAC has been working very hard in recent years to raise a substantial sum of money to buy a 99-year lease on the course. As I write this, I have just heard that they have hit their target, which is a brilliant achievement. The Trust is continuing to raise money to improve the hill's amenities for competitors and spectators, but we now know that the wonderful spectacle of hillclimbing at Shelsley has been preserved for us, and for future generations.

Reading Simon Taylor's book, I realise what a fascinating and varied history Shelsley Walsh has had over its first hundred years, starting from the days when the motor car was still a new-fangled contraption, and living on into today's very different times. It is good to know that Shelsley will still be the scene of friendly, yet fast and furious, hillclimbing competition one hundred years from now. That's what the Midland Automobile Club is determined to ensure, and I wish them every success.

London, Spring 2005

INTRODUCTION

Shelsley Walsh, the Midland Automobile Club's euphoniously-named speed hillclimb course in rural Worcestershire, is the oldest motorsport venue in continuous use in the world, bar none. It is older than Indianapolis, older than Le Mans, older than Monza. And, unlike any other car course that even approaches its age and standing, Shelsley is still being used almost without alteration.

It's not just the layout of the track that has remained the same. So, for much of its life, have the paddock shelters, the competitors' assembly area and the spectator banks. The very atmosphere of a Shelsley meeting is something rare: in an era when commercialism and big business have swamped almost every other area of motorsport, Shelsley Walsh still stands for sportsmanship, hard-fought but friendly contests, and racing purely for fun.

The cars have changed, of course. When Shelsley began, motoring was in its infancy, and the crude, bone-shaking machines entered took 80 seconds or more to cover the 1000 yards. Now the record is in the early 20s. Down the years some of the greatest cars and greatest drivers have appeared here: ERA and Mays, Auto Union and Stuck, Mercedes and Caracciola, Bugatti and Bugatti, BRM and Wharton, Cooper and Moss. They all led the way to today's super-sophisticated 650 horsepower single-seaters, whose brave drivers exceed 140mph up that same narrow, bumpy little lane.

I was first touched by the magic of Shelsley Walsh as a small child, reading reports in my father's old magazines of classic pre-war meetings. Within days of passing my driving test I got myself there as a teenage spectator, and instantly felt consumed by the place and its unique atmosphere. From the mid-1960s I went there as a working journalist, covering events for my then employer, *Autosport* magazine, talking to the drivers who took part and the officials who made it all happen. Eventually I found out what Shelsley was like for a competitor: an endlessly deceptive challenge, hugely demanding in terms of application, concentration and nerve, and an addiction that has proved hard to break.

OPPOSITE: Marshals at the ready as Barry Goodyear's Pilbeam rockets up to the Top Ess.

BELOW: Mark Joseland, 22 years MAC secretary and now club archivist, has long been loyal to the vintage Frazer Nash. This is Terror III at the Esses.

During a busy meeting, Midland AC secretary Roger Thomas (left) takes a breather with MAC chairman John Wood.

I now compete at Shelsley in my beloved 55-year-old sports-racing car, in which 400 horsepower and skinny tyres combine to keep my inexpert hands pretty full. You won't find my name in the record books, for there will always be competitors far more talented, and far braver, than me. But you will find me occupying one of the paddock bays, warming up the engine for my next climb, lining up at the bottom of the hill, or trying to get my breath back in the top paddock, just as often as the hard-pressed organisers will have me. To compete at any time at Shelsley is a privilege, because it allows you to become, for a weekend, just one tiny part of a living motorsport legend.

It is an even bigger privilege to have been asked to write Shelsley's history. I am grateful to the officers and directors of the Midland Automobile Club (MAC) who appointed me to that task, and to editorial director Mark Hughes and his colleagues at Haynes for feeling it might be worth publishing. I have had unstinting help from Midland AC secretary Roger Thomas, club president John Moody, club chairman John Wood, and a host of other Shelsley friends and experts, including among many others Paul

Long-time Shelsley addicts: (from left) Terry Grainger, Howard Stockley and Bob Cooper indulge in paddock gossip, while six-times British champion Tony Marsh listens.

Matty, Jeremy Bouckley, Terry Grainger and Robin Mynett. The erudite Howard Stockley used his encyclopaedic knowledge of the hill to put me straight on many matters, always with patience and good humour. I would never have started on the book without the encouragement of long-time Shelsley competitor and good friend Richard Drewett. And I could not have completed it without being able to consult the true historian of hillclimbing, Chris Mason, whose indispensable work *Uphill Racers* is the best book on the sport ever written.

Most of all, I must offer my thanks to Mark Joseland, the indefatigable and hugely knowledgeable keeper of the Shelsley Walsh archives. Mark has been going to Shelsley since he was a small boy, and has competed there for more than 40 years, nowadays in his wonderful and historic Frazer Nash, *Terror III*. He has taken endless time and trouble to find many of the wonderful photographs in this book, to confirm or deny historical facts and fancies, and act as a constant source of encouragement.

The photographs have come from a variety of sources, and a study of the acknowledgements list will show that the work of several stalwart Shelsley photographers features strongly. The wonderful LAT archive provided many truly historic shots, thanks to the patience and enthusiasm of Peter Higham and his team.

But in particular I must offer my thanks to Roger McDonald, who has been taking photographs at Shelsley Walsh for almost half a century, using mainly his beloved Linhof Technica. Many of his photographs were taken specially for this book.

Finally, there is a debt of gratitude that we all owe. With the expiry of the current lease in 2004, it seemed that hillclimbing at Shelsley Walsh would end for ever. Over £1 million was needed for a new 99-year lease: a daunting task. Under its president John Moody, the MAC met the challenge by setting up a Trust, chaired by Martyn Griffiths. Over more than two years of relentless effort, and thanks to the generosity of club members, competitors and the public, the money was raised. The new lease was signed in March 2005, and the hill is now secure until 2103. Thanks to the Trust's dedicated work, we can all go on enjoying the most famous hillclimb in the world.

The author trying to follow the experts' line through Crossing. His historic 1950/56 HWM-Chevrolet, the Stovebolt Special, has climbed Shelsley in 35.49sec.

THE ATMOSPHERE OF SHELSLEY

The green hills and valleys of rural Worcestershire contain some of England's most beautiful countryside. Running diagonally through the county is the River Teme, an angler's delight of brown trout and grayling and barbel, which begins as a spring on Cilfaesty Hill in mid-Wales and flows through Shropshire and Herefordshire to meet the Severn in the county town of Worcester. Tranquil villages, little changed for hundreds of years, are scattered along the river valley and cling to the sides of its rolling slopes. Strung out on a narrow byway between two of those villages, Stanford Bridge and Martley, are the three tiny hamlets of Shelsley Kings, Shelsley Beauchamp and Shelsley Walsh.

Two of the Shelsleys are virtually unknown outside the county, but the third is a household name to motorsport enthusiasts around the globe. That's because it has given its name to the world's oldest motorsport venue, which after a century is still being used in precisely its original layout. On a few weekends during the year, crowds of 10,000 or more are drawn to the Teme Valley to see a pure form of motorsport which is itself almost unique – because it has resolutely remained true to its origins, and has kept itself unspoiled by the commercial pressures and big money that have turned most of modern motor racing from a sport into a business.

So Shelsley Walsh means not just the hamlet – the few haphazard cottages, the farmyard surrounding the 16th century Court House, the tiny Church of St Andrew which dates back to the 12th century. It also means the hillclimb, the steep, snaking 1000 yards of narrow lane which runs from the farmyard, twists up through the woods and then bursts onto the open pastureland above.

Arriving at 7 o'clock on a Sunday morning in the paddock at the bottom of the hill, the loudest sound is birdsong, the dominant aroma one of fresh coffee and bacon from the competitors' campsite on the other side of the lane. Sheltering in the covered paddock bays after the previous day's practice sessions are some 150 cars of astonishing variety: primitive vintage specials,

OPPOSITE: The Worcestershire countryside provides a truly English backdrop for the Shelsley Walsh hillclimb.

BELOW: St Andrew's Church, and the Court House beyond.

The spectators' car park is always worth a look. This is a fine line-up of vintage Vauxhalls.

standard-looking production sports cars, serious racing cars from the recent past, ultra-modern single-seaters with Formula 1 engines and state of the art aerodynamics.

Soon the paddock comes to life as drivers and helpers fettle their machinery, exchanging wild tales of Saturday's runs, swapping gossip and tools and friendly advice. At 9am the little church on the edge of the paddock holds its morning service, and among the congregation are usually a few sets of oily overalls and brightly coloured fireproof race suits. The service over, engines start to burst into noisy life, warming up for the first runs which start at 10am.

For an hour or more the spectators' cars have been queuing to get into the steep field which forms the side of the hill. The automotive variety in the car park almost rivals the paddock, for enthusiasts love to get out their own cherished vintage or classic car and make a day trip to Shelsley. Along the hedge separating the car park

from the track, specialist dealers have set up temporary shops, selling old motor racing books and magazines, hillclimb memorabilia and photos, and even film posters from movies whose plots featured the motor car. Knots of spectators are toiling up the field towards the wooded glade above the Esses, where rustic benches are set in angled tiers to provide excellent viewing and the perfect spot to lighten a picnic hamper. There are vantage points along the entire 1000 yards, all the way up to the fast, narrow straight at the top and the finishing paddock.

Promptly at 10am a briskly efficient marshal, who is on first-name terms with all the regular competitors, waves forward the first car in the queue that has assembled at the front of the paddock. It's a workmanlike Caterham Seven, gleaming after hours of careful preparation and the ideal hillclimb weapon: light, powerful, quick handling and comparatively inexpensive.

Approaching the startline the driver aggressively

spins his rear wheels to ensure the tyres are as warm, and as clean, as possible before moving up to the line. A small vertical strut, painted black, is fixed onto the front of every hillclimb car: this is to break the timing light beams at the bottom and the top of the hill, so that every climb can be timed consistently to a hundredth of a second. One startline marshal lines up the strut with the timing beam, another puts a chock under the rear wheel so the car will not roll back. Both officials, very necessarily, wear ear defenders: hillclimb cars, especially as they leave the line, can be ear-damagingly loud.

The light to the driver's left goes green. He lowers his visor, builds the revs to the ideal combination of power and traction and, when he is ready, moves his left foot off the clutch.

At once the car is launched up the steep, narrow strip of tarmac with a howling roar from the exhaust and a shriek from the spinning tyres. As the driver snatches second gear, almost at once there is a deceptively sharp left-hand corner – Kennel Bend. Then a brief, steeply rising straight to another corner – The Crossing – not so sharp, but he's going more quickly now, and the road runs between high banks here so there is no margin for error. Then the road curves slightly to the left, and there is a nasty dip which uses up the little Caterham's suspension travel and makes the chassis thump on the road in a shower of sparks.

He's doing over 90mph now, and rushing at him dead ahead is the beckoning earth bank which describes the outside of the Bottom Ess. Brake too late and he's in the bank, brake too early and he loses too much speed, for the gradient here is at its steepest. He judges it just

Pre-event briefing for the dedicated posse of marshals and medical staff. No hillclimb could run without them.

The start-line marshal lines up Dave Wilson's 2-litre Caterham with the timing beam.

right, off the brake, snatch second gear and hard left for the Bottom Ess, skittering on the edge of adhesion. At once he swings back across the road to turn sharp right for the Top Ess, where a deep drain cover almost at the apex is ready to bounce the car across the road. Then the banks and the overhanging trees are left behind, and the road runs steep and straight between open fields towards the horizon. Up through the gears, our man's little Caterham screams to almost 100 miles an hour as it flashes under the banner that marks the finish line. Barely half a minute has elapsed since it left the start line, but for the driver a whole lot of concentrated living on the edge has been crammed into those thirty seconds.

Immediately there is the problem of getting the car stopped, for with alarming rapidity the tarmac gives way to grass and an emergency gravel trap. Having achieved that, the driver swings right across the grass to stop in a holding area, switching his engine into silence and able to relax while the rest of his classmates give their best up the hill. Then, because Shelsley Walsh has no return road, they all coast back down the hill to the paddock and their respective bays. The drivers re-run in their

mind's eye the climb they have just made, yard by yard. They try to analyse how their second attempt later in the day can be just a bit quicker, and – like any angler – tell their team of helpers about the new class record that, somehow, got away.

In Shelsley's early days, all each competitor ever knew was his or her elapsed time from start line to finish line. With today's sophisticated electronic equipment, there are four further bits of information. A light beam just after the start measures the elapsed time for the first 64 feet. Getting the start right is vital, for with a powerful car precious fractions can be lost, using too much power and indulging in too much wasteful wheelspin, or dropping the clutch at revs that are too low and missing the peak of the car's torque curve. Gravity accelerates an object at 32 feet per second per second, so a first 64-foot time of two seconds betters 1g. Some of the fastest cars have managed under 1.9sec.

A further pair of lights records a car's speed just before it brakes for the Esses, and also the elapsed time to that point. So, if a run is disappointing, the driver can establish whether he lost time in the lower or upper half of the hill.

The start: black rubber lines from others' spinning wheels point the way.

Kennel: sharper than it looks. Some ease the throttle, some take it flat.

Crossing approach: The slight kink to the right is no reason to lift, so stay hard on the power.

Crossing: the grass banks close in. It's deceptively sharp: keep to the right to ease the line.

The Kink: flat out here, but there's a big bump at the apex, which can throw your car off-line to the right. This is 130mph in a big single-seater.

Bottom Ess: it's all about where to brake, but reference points are hard to find. Too early and you're slow, too late and you're in the bank – hard.

Top Ess: swing to the left to approach this right-hander. Taking a later apex will give you more safety margin coming out.

Top Straight: from now on it's all about horsepower, and clean upward gear-changes.

Finish line: you mustn't lift until you're under the banner, even though that brow is dauntingly blind. The big boys are doing over 140mph.

Braking area: suddenly tarmac becomes bumpy concrete, and then grass, so you have to brake really hard.

And at the top, as well as the total time, the beams at the finish record the speed over the finish line.

A team of highly knowledgeable course commentators, stationed at three points up the hill, have an instant read-out of all this information. They describe each stage of each climb, keeping the crowd fully informed about the pedigree of the car and driver, and announce the times and speeds achieved. The meeting is run at a brisk pace. As soon as a car has left the Esses the lights at the bottom turn green, so two cars can run on the hill at once – although the orange-overalled marshals up the hill can quickly red-flag the second car if the first one has come to grief. The entire programme is run through twice: thus every car gets two climbs during the day, even though for the major meetings nearly 200 cars may be entered. With a century of experience, the Midland Automobile Club have become very adept at running things efficiently. Their faithful team of highly qualified and hard-working helpers – clerks of the course, marshals, timekeepers, stewards, scrutineers and medical staff – know their respective jobs perfectly. Bad weather, accidents and mechanical mishaps can all conspire to throw the schedule off course, but Shelsley always seems to run like clockwork.

Two of the major meetings each year are rounds of the British Hillclimb Championship, which is fought out by the nation's best hillclimb drivers and fastest hillclimb cars at venues all over the British Isles. The fastest 12 cars from the first runs qualify for the Top Twelve run-off, for which championship points are awarded – 10 points for fastest down to one point for tenth fastest. An additional point can be earned for beating the outright record for the hill. After all the second runs, the same process happens again.

Students of Shelsley Walsh can trace the gradual reduction of the hill record, from 77.6 seconds at the first meeting in 1905 down to Raymond Mays' "magic time" of 37.37sec a few weeks before World War II broke out. With the onward march of racing car design the times went on getting shorter, but it wasn't until 1971 that half a minute was beaten. As each new barrier fell – into the 27s in 1976, into the 26s in 1980, incredibly into the 25s in 1990 – it always seemed that it would be a physical impossibility for a car to climb this hill any quicker. The next full second took 12 years to come off, but in 2002 Graeme Wight Junior and his V6 Gould

GR51 broke 25 seconds with a simply sensational 24.85. It defied the imagination to think that anybody was ever going to dip below 24.

But the fractions continued to be shaved away, and only two years later, on 15 August 2004, came a truly memorable climb. The very talented, very brave Adam Fleetwood, a red-haired lad who shares his mighty 3.5-litre V8 Gould GR55 with his father Roger, rocketed up the hill to write another chapter in Shelsley's history. I was watching this climb from the bank above the Esses approach, and the car seemed to bound over the bumps almost faster than the eye could follow. Adam's speed into the Esses, just before he came off the power and hit the brakes as that bank loomed, was a frightening 133 miles an hour – on a piece of undulating lane that seemed barely wider than the car itself. Through the Bottom Ess the Gould seemed to defy physics, staying glued to its line as Adam powered round the left-hander with awe-inspiring commitment, on around the steep right-hander and out of sight. Around me, knowledgeable spectators said "Phew" and "Wow" and shook their heads in disbelief. One lady shuddered.

Then the loudspeakers told us the time: Twenty-three point eight-seven seconds. The 24-second barrier had been well and truly breached. The crowd erupted into delighted cheers, repeated a few minutes later as the Gould coasted silently down the hill, with young Adam modestly acknowledging the applause. His speed over the finish line, just before that worryingly short braking area, had been 142 miles per hour.

Every bit as entertaining as watching the cars on the hill is wandering around the paddock, looking at the machinery and meeting the people. Hillclimb folk are friendly, and usually delighted to chat to passers-by about their cars and their sport. These days, in the higher echelons of motor racing, the ordinary public can't get into the paddock at any price: they are shut out. At lesser events you can get into the paddock if you pay a substantial extra fee. At Shelsley your admission ticket allows you in among the cars and the drivers without question, because that is part of the reason why you came.

The Shelsley atmosphere is relaxed and good-humoured – and yet, when it comes to your climb, it suddenly becomes deadly serious. The fascination of this sport is that the same challenge applies to every competitor, however humble the

Denis Jenkinson prepares for his run astride his faithful TriBsa, August 1990.

mount, however inexperienced the driver. Whether you are Adam Fleetwood, or a newcomer in a Mini or Sprite, it is the same: your rival is the clock. It doesn't matter if you drive the slowest car in your class and everyone else is streets ahead of you. If your best ever time up Shelsley is 45 seconds and the day comes when you manage a 44.9, you feel like you've just won a Grand Prix.

Denis Jenkinson, motorsport journalist and co-driver supreme, who navigated Stirling Moss to victory in the 1955 Mille Miglia, liked to spend his free weekends riding his aged TriBsa motorbike up Shelsley. Try as he might, Jenks could never quite break 40 seconds. But finally, not many years before his death, after a winter of fettling and with a real do-or-die effort, he managed a time of 39.75sec. He reckoned it was the best day of his life, and he was only half-joking when he said the Mille Miglia win paled into insignificance beside it.

When the long day's sport is over, with its triumphs and disappointments, its quiet successes and frustrating failures, there is an informal prize-giving halfway up the hill. For the accolade of Best Time of Day (BTD) there is a cheque and a trophy; class winners are later sent a small engraved cup as a memento of their exploits. The spectators go home happy, talking of new records and near misses, and the efforts of their particular favourites. Cars are loaded onto trailers and into vans, or have their race numbers peeled off and hoods erected, if they have them, for the drive home – for some, as far as Western Cornwall or the North of Scotland. The hard-worked officials tidy the paddock area, take down the signs, close the canteen and empty the litter bins. The hamlet on the hill above the Teme settles back to the quiet, slow-moving rural existence it has followed for hundreds of years…until the next Shelsley Walsh Hillclimb.

You can hillclimb just about any type of vehicle at Shelsley Walsh, from a 1956 Maserati 250F Grand Prix car (Chris Drake gets away from the start, above) to a humble road-going Mini (Terry Healy, left, at Kennel).

THE BEGINNINGS 1905–1913

The elderly Queen Victoria still reigned over her Empire when the industrial areas of central England began to emerge as the home of Britain's fledgling motor industry. The bicycle boom had been good to the Midlands, and now several of the new autocar makers had set up shop in the Birmingham and Coventry areas. On 11 January 1901, just 11 days before the old queen died, a group of local businessmen gathered at the Grand Hotel in Birmingham to discuss the foundation of a Midland Automobile Club. Local car manufacturers among those inaugural members included Herbert Austin, then running Wolseley but soon to found his own car company; the redoubtable Lanchester brothers, Fred, Frank and George; and J.D. Siddeley, who through Siddeley-Deasey, Armstrong-Siddeley and Hawker-Siddeley was to be a figure in both the motor and aircraft industries. Also present was Henry Sturmey, who five years earlier had founded Britain's first car magazine, *The Autocar*.

To begin with, the new club's calendar was mainly social. But, inevitably, the temptation among some members to compete against one another in their motor cars became impossible to resist. One of the earliest forms of motoring contest was the hillclimb, at first more a demonstration of a car's ability (or otherwise) to get to the top of a steep slope than a test of speed. On 5 October 1901 the MAC held its first hillclimb at Gorcott Hill, on the main Birmingham-Alcester road. No times or speeds were published, but the fastest car was acknowledged to be A.E. Crowdy's

In Shelsley's early days, more passengers meant more weight, and thus a better handicap. During the 1906 meeting, J.A. Doran's 22hp Minerva arrives at the Esses in a cloud of dust with a full complement of well-wrapped Edwardian gentlemen hanging on tight. Its time of 150.4sec was 14th BTD.

12 August 1905: Ernest Instone and his passengers approach the top of the hill to take their place in motorsport history with Shelsley's first BTD in 77.6sec.

8hp Darracq. After more events there and at Weatheroak Hill, just outside Birmingham, a sterner test was found at Edge Hill in Warwickshire.

Better known as Sun Rising Hill, this 1000-yard venue had several acute corners and gradients as steep as 1 in 6.25, and the rules called for two mandatory stop-starts on the way up. Cecil Edge's Napier won the first Sun Rising event, although there were mutterings that it used a works racing engine despite being entered in the touring car class – shades of a later era of motorsport. Other names on the entry list included Herbert Austin (Wolseley), George Lanchester (Lanchester) and the Hon Charles Rolls (Panhard – he had yet to be introduced to Henry Royce). Although successful, the three events run at Sun Rising Hill between July 1903 and July 1904 were blighted by police speed traps – the legal limit was still 12mph – and by a disgruntled local farmer. *The Autocar* reported: "A gentleman who signs himself 'Esq', resident in the locality, who does not approve of motor cars, signified his disapproval by causing his manure carts to be driven up and down the hill most of the afternoon."

So the club committee resolved to find a venue on private ground, and in June 1905 an event was held on an estate road at Middle Hill, Broadway. But already something potentially much better had been discovered. The club treasurer, Cedric Type, was accountant to the local branch of the Farmers' Union, and had a wide knowledge of the surrounding countryside. He knew of a farm in the Teme Valley which had a steep bridle path connecting two parts of the property. He tackled the farmer, Montagu Taylor, and Taylor, who was already an MAC member, pronounced himself willing to co-operate. With astonishing speed the track was widened, a rough gravel surface laid, fences erected and undergrowth cleared to accommodate spectators. On Saturday 12 August 1905, 39 cars took part in the first Shelsley Walsh hillclimb.

For most of its length the hill had a steep bank rising on one side, making a perfect natural grandstand. As they clambered up to their chosen vantage point, spectators could enjoy impressive views across the rolling valley, for this was rural Worcestershire at its best. At the bottom of the hill was the substantial Court House, where Squire Taylor lived, plus farm buildings, the tiny country church and an attractive half-timbered cottage. From the farmyard the track ran around a left-hand bend, then steeply upwards around a second left-hander. A short straight led to a sharp left and right under overhanging trees, before emerging through a gateway into open land again, with a steep straight to the crest of the hill. Total length was 992 yards.

The weather for that first meeting was fine and warm. Among the spectators, who were not charged for admission, was a young man called Leslie Wilson. He cannot have guessed how inextricably his life was to become linked with the hill, for 16 years later he was appointed MAC club secretary, and he went on to hold the post for 37 years until 1958. His eyewitness account captures the atmosphere of the occasion.

On arrival at Shelsley we had a grand time inspecting the cars and talking to the drivers, most of whom, being 'racing' drivers, were the motoring personalities of the day. Miss Larkins and her lady passenger were lying underneath their 6hp Wolseley, preparing for the fray. And in the car park I had not seen such an *assembly of cars of different makes and types in one place other than at the Motor Show, and we revelled in examining every detail of them.*

The old cart shed had been whitewashed out and decorated with flowers and farm produce. Long trestle tables laden with food lined each side, with competitors and members enjoying a marvellous lunch waited upon by waiters in full regalia. The colossal beef steak puddings were quite two foot six in diameter, all piping hot and most appetising. The Worcester Civil Military Band dispensed music in the farmyard.

Excitement was now rising amongst the ladies and gentlemen lining the road on both sides, arrayed in their summer frocks and suitings. Amongst the sporting men, very tight stovepipe trousers and extremely high collars and bow ties were the vogue. Straw brimmers and caps predominated, with a few of the very motor-minded in leather breeches and leggings.

Frederick Coleman with the White that set Shelsley's only steam-powered BTD in 1906.

The road was made up of gravel, well rolled, which became terribly dusty in the dry weather. The event was controlled by a kind of bush telegraph. Hand bells were placed at certain points and rung by policemen as the cars passed their posts, so the spectators more or less knew the position of each car on the hill. No 1 bell was rung as the car started from the line, and No 6 bell was at the finish line, so if you wanted to time a car yourself you did it from the first to the last bell. No 5 was on the top bend of the S, an extra large ship's bell behind the hedge and very, very loud and deafening, which told the officials at the start that the car had passed successfully and another car could be got to the line.

Altogether it was a very delightfully combined picnic and hill climb, the weather was perfect

E.J. Blakemore's little 10hp Allday on the Martley weighbridge in 1907 complete with three passengers. Thus laden, his climb took 198.2sec.

and everybody knew everybody. At the end of the 39 runs – only one for each car – we drifted back to the rickyard where tea was laid out.

Two major trophies were offered at that first meeting: for the fastest climb, and for the overall winner "on Formula of Merit", a handicap which took account of vehicle weight, including passengers. To establish this, all competitors were required to visit the public weighbridge in the nearby village of Martley. Cars of over 20hp had to have four-seater bodies and carry a full complement of passengers. The fastest climb was achieved by Ernest Instone in a 35 horsepower Daimler, climbing in 1 minute 17.6 seconds, and the slowest by Guilding's De Dion in 6 minutes 34.4 seconds. At least he got to the top: the very first car to attempt the hill, the Motobloc 10-12 of W. M. Hawnt, was stopped by the gradient less

LEFT: Sydney Smith in the 40hp Napier entered in 1907 by S.F. Edge. This big car climbed in 92.6sec to set eighth BTD.

BELOW: L. Meek's 10hp Allday at the start, one of six at the 1907 meeting. It took a steady 266.4sec to reach the top of the hill.

than halfway up. During the afternoon three more failed to make it. But the biggest accolade, and the President's Cup, went to the winner on formula, G. Patterson in G.F. Heath's single-cylinder De Dion.

In becoming the first Shelsley record holder, Ernest Instone began a long family relationship with the hill. After a spell as manager of the Daimler Motor Co, he set up Stratton & Instone which, as Stratstones of Mayfair, continued to be a London Daimler dealership, and still exists as part of the Pendragon Motor Group almost a century later. His son Rupert was a prolific hillclimber from the 1930s to the 1950s in a succession of Shelsley Specials, and in 2001 the half-timbered cottage opposite the farmyard was purchased and restored by Pendragon.

After that successful first meeting, the Shelsley Walsh Hillclimb was held annually up until the outbreak of World War I. News of Shelsley soon spread beyond the Midlands, and the entry lists began to include names already famous, and soon to be famous, in the motoring world: Charles Jarrott, Louis Coatalen, Victor Riley, H.F.S. Morgan, Cecil Bianchi, Roy Fedden, W.O. Bentley.

J.A. Holder's 25hp Calthorpe set fourth BTD in 1909 in 87.4sec.

There were society names too: Viscount Ingestre, Gerald von Stralendorff, Dorothy Levitt, the Maharajah of Tikari.

In 1906, in indifferent weather, fastest time was set by a steam car, the White of Frederick Coleman. The slowest, by Luff-Smith's 800cc Wolseley, occupied 10 minutes 1.6 seconds, which to this day remains an unbeaten record for worst uninterrupted time of day. The following year the finish line was moved eight yards further up the final straight to make the distance exactly 1000 yards, and at the same time the steep rise between the two first left-handers was eased by digging a cutting, which helped J.E. Hutton's 80 horsepower Berliet to take more than 10sec off Instone's two-year-old record. For the 1908 event a cement dressing improved the dusty surface, and H.C. Tryon's 60-horse Napier lowered the record further, to 65.4sec. By now the corners had assumed names: the first left-hander became Kennel Bend, because of its proximity to the dog

kennels where the local hunt pack was housed. Spectators could cross the track near the second left-hander, so that became The Crossing. The left and right inevitably became the Esses, later distinguished as Bottom Ess and Top Ess.

In 1909 H.C. Holder set the first of three consecutive fastest times with his mighty 58hp Daimler, but this year and the next he was well off Tryon's record. Shelsley Walsh had by now become a major national motoring event, and was treated as such by the car magazines, which reported it in blow-by-blow detail in the charmingly overblown prose of the period. This is a typical excerpt from *The Motor* report of the 1911 meeting:

When the bell rang to signal the approach of the next car, there was a buzz of excitement, as, on glancing at the programme, one saw that the car expected was likely to be a lively one, and, moreover, was in the hands of a very skilful

ABOVE: H.C. Holder sets off on his record-breaking 1911 climb with the big 58hp Daimler. He brought the record down to 62.2sec.

LEFT: A.J. Hancock's passenger works hard at Crossing to improve lateral weight distribution. Their Prince Henry Vauxhall was the 1911 winner on formula with 72.0sec.

ABOVE: The hired weighbridge in the Shelsley paddock in 1912 with Arthur Cox's Riley 12/18 aboard. The car behind is a Briton, built in Wolverhampton.

BELOW: Joseph Higginson's triumphant final run in 1913 with his new Vauxhall, minus passengers, occupied just 55.2sec. His record was to stand until after World War I.

spectators from the track, and we were treated to the pièce de résistance – the record-breaking ascent of Mr H.C. Holder's 58hp Daimler to wit. He came up in magnificent style, but took the first corner of the 'S' bend (in the writer's opinion) just a trifle too late for the speed of the car, and had a bad rear-wheel skid, which, however, was very cleverly corrected.

Holder's time with the big Daimler on that run was 63.4 seconds, and was indeed a new record. In fact he managed 62.2 seconds later the same day, for as an MAC member he could run both in the open competition and the closed members' class. But because no practice was allowed, the club would only accept a driver's first time as a record: a second run was thought to confer an unfair advantage.

When the cars had finished, a healthy entry of motorcycles took over the hill under the auspices of the Birmingham Motor Cycle Club. Fastest time was set by Moorhouse's Indian in a remarkable 55.6sec, although this is not comparable with the car times because the bikes were allowed a flying start some 30 yards before the start line.

There were concerns among MAC members at this point about the future of the hill, because the Court House Farm estate was up for sale. But happily the new owner, T.L. Walker, JP, proved to be just as benign towards the club's annual visit as his predecessor. Spectators were still admitted free of charge, and the crowds were now considerable. *The Motor* reckoned the turnout compared favourably with the new seat of motor racing south-west of London: "In comparison with the average Brooklands meeting, there must have been half as many cars again parked in the enclosures or lined up along the roads outside". Of course there was still no public address commentary, although competitors' times were chalked on boards at intervals up the hill, and in his hut in the paddock "Secretary Type gave out encyclopaedic information to a never-ending stream of spectators". The system of bells had been augmented by a primitive field telephone, and a hired weighbridge in the paddock avoided the need for entrants to be weighed in Martley. This must have made difficulties for the man who allegedly improved his handicap by installing a hidden water tank in the chassis of his car which, after the weighing, unobtrusively disgorged its contents on the road from Martley back to Shelsley.

driver. The cause of the cloud of dust which we could now see approaching was Mr Percy Kidner's 15.9hp Vauxhall, driven by Mr A.J. Hancock, and he took the corner so fast that he had a bad front-wheel skid, almost instantaneously followed by a similar disconcerting piece of misbehaviour on the part of the rear wheels – no doubt out of sympathy with the front ones; but both these peccadilloes were splendidly checked by Mr Hancock before he got to the second bend, round which he went in fine style, to the accompaniment of well-merited applause.

Once again that ominous tintinnabulation of the bell, and a general scattering of the

Sunbeam designer Louis Coatalen on the line in 1913 with the special 25/30 racer with V8 Sunbeam Crusader aero engine. In the same car Chris Bird climbed in an impressive 58.4sec.

Making his first visit to Shelsley for the 1912 meeting was a wealthy Lancashire businessman called Joseph Higginson, who had already had some success in Northern events with his mighty 13.6-litre La Buire. He set Best Time of Day – but he was 5.4 seconds off Holder's record. Consumed, as so many would be after him, by the elusive challenge of those steep 1000 yards, he decided to commission a car specifically to suit the narrow hill better than the La Buire. After talking to several manufacturers he ordered Laurence Pomeroy Sr to build him a special Vauxhall, a lightened version of their Coupe de l'Auto car with a 4.7-litre engine. It was to be the prototype of the immortal Vauxhall 30/98.

For the 1913 event, Shelsley took on a new aspect. The latest RAC regulations permitted racing bodies and freer modifications for the bigger machinery, so effectively proper racing cars were allowed for the first time. As a result, works cars were officially entered or tacitly blessed by Talbot, Crossley, DFP and Sunbeam, who brought an eight-cylinder, 6-litre aero-engined car. But Higginson and his new car were indomitable. He managed to fit in three runs, first in the open category, carrying a full complement of passengers, then in the team event representing the Lancashire Automobile Club, and finally in the closed event. During the day several others bettered Holder's record, but on his final run Higginson got down to a brilliant 55.2 seconds. This was two seconds clear of the next fastest car, Leslie Hands' works Talbot, and a full eight seconds under the old record. Only a driver's first run could officially count as a record, and thus Hands was declared the scratch winner of the event. But this time was generally accepted by Shelsley enthusiasts as the new mark. According to one report:

The patently outstanding performance was the meteoric display of Mr Higginson, who beat the poor old existing record so badly that we think the time will stand as the fastest climb for some considerable time. It must be nearly the limit without taking undue risks of an accident.

Higginson's time did indeed stand for eight years, for the following summer the world was plunged into the biggest, bloodiest conflict it had ever known. The Midland Automobile Club busied itself with raising funds for an ambulance for the French Red Cross, and Shelsley Walsh fell silent for the duration of the Great War.

THE VINTAGE YEARS 1920–1929

It wasn't until July 1920 that Shelsley Walsh echoed once more to the sound of hillclimbing. Announcing the forthcoming event, *The Motor* reckoned "the revival is one of the pleasurable indications of our return to peacetime conditions". One of their writers visited the old course, finding that after the long lay-off "it is a mass of loose stones and shingle. But the MAC has requisitioned a steam roller, so that the surface should be in perfect condition for the event".

Nevertheless the entry was a mere 33 cars. The exorbitant entry fee of 20 guineas (reduced in later years) was at least a month's salary for an ordinary man, and for that sum the competitors got just one go at the hill. It was dry for the first few climbs, but then a ferocious thunderstorm brought the meeting to a temporary halt and left the loose track muddy and slippery. At that point Christopher Bird's blue-grey 4.9-litre Indianapolis Sunbeam was fastest from a rather battered-looking Clement-Talbot driven by Lieutenant A. Vandervell – the same Tony Vandervell who, 38 years later, saw his patriotic team of Vanwall Grand Prix cars bring the first Formula 1 Constructors' World Championship to Britain. Both had their run before the storm, although young Vandervell's ascent was by all accounts pretty wild. Passengers were of course still permitted, and some behaved with as much enthusiasm as bouncers in a trial:

Vandervell's Talbot was equipped with a four-seater body in which was one passenger in the back seat, flinging himself from side to side at the most exciting moments during the skidding, possibly with some idea of moving his weight to correct matters. As the car flashed along the finishing straight the head of the passenger must have been in the seat cushion, for both his legs were clearly visible in the air.

In the treacherous conditions the other competitors were naturally much slower. But towards the end of the wet, dank afternoon came a significant climb which pointed the way towards a crucial new philosophy for lightweight, no-compromise hillclimb machinery. According to *The Autocar*, "Captain Archie Frazer-Nash's car looked like a tin whistle at the front and a queer sort of fish at the back, but a wonderfully game fellow to go" and later referred to it in full cry as "an infuriated reptile". *The Motor* reporter, slipping from past to present tense in his excitement, described the run thus:

People looked at their programmes. "Captain Nash on his racing GN", they murmured, and drew a little closer to the hedges. Below we heard the sharp cackle of a well-tuned twin. Then, at what seemed terrific speed, he burst into view. The first bend he took fairly close, but his tail swung out, the soft ground failing to hold his narrow tyres. Cleverly straightening, he hurtles up to the right-hander, cuts out for a second, swoops round and is flying up to the finish. He made second fastest time of day.

A famous shot by The Motor's photographer of Basil Davenport and Spider in full cry, sliding out of the Bottom Ess in September 1929. After six consecutive BTDs, Basil was vanquished this time by Mays in the Vauxhall Villiers.

Archie Frazer-Nash in his GN Moldy, which set second BTD in 1920 and effectively pioneered the philosophy of the small, manoeuvrable hillclimb car.

In wet conditions, the GN had beaten Vandervell's dry time, and got within 1.8 sec of Bird. It had set the stage for generations of small, light hillclimb cars to come, from Basil Davenport's Spiders via the V-twin Coopers of the 1950s to the modern equivalent using multi-cylinder Japanese motorcycle engines. In equal conditions Frazer-Nash would certainly have set Best Time of Day.

Despite the weather and the small entry, the first post-war meeting had been a great success. The large crowd of spectators were still admitted free, although there was a one-shilling charge for parking, with AA scouts manning the car parks. By the time the meeting was over the fields had become bogs, and carthorses had to be brought in to drag out stranded cars. The only press criticism concerned the behaviour of spectators, who were permitted to walk on the course during the meeting to find a good vantage point. Many, said *The Autocar*, "seemed bent on suicide". But the future of the Shelsley Walsh

venue appeared secure, especially as Squire Walker was a keen motorist. In his well-equipped garage beside the Court House he kept a Sunbeam and a Morgan three-wheeler, and he seemed to welcome the annual influx of hillclimbers. Less secure was the position of the Midland Automobile Club itself. Despite the high entry fees, each event had made a loss, and club funds were running very low.

But then the dedicated, meticulous Leslie Wilson took over as secretary of the club, drafting his sister Doris onto the strength as his assistant. Wilson was to rule at Shelsley until 1958, by which time he had overseen some 60 meetings. He later claimed that on his appointment, when he first looked at the club accounts, he found there was a credit of precisely 7s 6d (37.5p) in the bank. Obviously drastic measures were called for, and one of his first moves was to recommend to the committee that spectators should be charged for admission – but only the men, for it was deemed ungentlemanly to charge ladies. No prior announcement was made, so the 5000-strong crowd that turned up on this warm September Saturday only found out they had to pay when they arrived at the gate. But clearly a substantial profit was made, which impelled *The Autocar* to resort to unfamiliar criticism, clothed in heavy irony:

Ladies were admitted free, but the club extracted five shillings from each male visitor, and charged a shilling for a not too informative programme. Without in any way wishing to speak derogatively of the sporting character of the event, one feels fairly confident that one may congratulate the Midland AC on making a very successful affair from the financial point of view.

It was again Chris Bird who set BTD. This time, in perfect conditions and clouds of dust, the Sunbeam – now wearing long-tailed single-seater bodywork – took an impressive 3sec off Higginson's eight-year record. Archie Frazer-Nash's GN *Kim* easily took the light car class once more, but was pushed out of second place overall by a Shelsley newcomer, Matthew Park, driving a 1914 Grand Prix Vauxhall. Shocked by the speeds, the curmudgeonly man from *The Autocar* struck a reproving note:

The hill is not safe for the fastest cars. The bends are too acute, the road is too narrow to allow a driver much chance to recover himself if he gets into difficulties. The pull-up is too short, and is flanked by a pair of narrow-set gateposts which ought to be

Chris Bird on the startline in 1921 with the single-seater Indianapolis Sunbeam before breaking the hill record.

Officials of the meeting,
1922: (from left)
timekeeper George
Reynolds, judge Cedric
Type, steward A.G.
Johnson and wife, club
president W. Ballin Hinde,
and secretary Leslie
Wilson.

removed. To speak plainly, the hill does not provide a test of a car, but rather of the driver. The Shelsley bends put too much of a premium on recklessness, and one or two of the competing cars were very near indeed to getting completely out of hand.

But none of this sniping could halt Shelsley's relentless progress. It continued to go from strength to strength, and was now seen by many car manufacturers as an event too important to ignore. Equally, a driver who wanted to make his name knew that a good climb at Shelsley was an excellent way to demonstrate his potential.

For the 1922 meeting the spectator attendance was estimated at 7000, with 2000 cars parked in the fields at the foot of the hill. Wilson's efforts saw to it that the notorious gateway beyond the finish line was widened, although the farmer would not allow it to be removed completely. A

big board at the Esses, manned by boy scouts, displayed the times achieved by each competitor to help the crowd follow the fun. A minor piece of history was made when Louis Kings ascended in 89.8s in an Austin Seven: it was the car's competition debut. More than eighty years later, the Austin Seven was still providing scores of enthusiasts with a cheap and enjoyable way to go racing.

Matt Park's works TT Vauxhall took BTD by a fifth of a second after Bird's Sunbeam had a big sideways moment at the Bottom Ess, bouncing off both banks. Archie Frazer-Nash was another to hit the bank: he buckled two wheels and burst a front tyre, but carried on to the finish on the rim. Then towards the end of the afternoon he and Count Louis Zborowski (straight-eight Grand Prix Ballot) challenged each other to a match, and somehow got past the start line marshals to take second climbs. The organisers were furious, refused to

Archie Frazer-Nash and Leon Cushman toil up the hill with a fresh wheel for the GN after it had hit the Esses bank in 1922.

Zborowski's Grand Prix Ballot storms the hill in 1922. Note the spectators on both sides of the road: from 1925 one side was closed to the public.

announce the times achieved, and banned both men from competing the following year – although in Frazer-Nash's case at least, the punishment was clearly forgotten, for he was back at Shelsley in 1923.

And 1922 marked the rise of one of the big Shelsley Walsh names, a driver who would set BTD more than 20 times over the next 26 years and go on to become a major player in motorsport as a whole. Raymond Mays had first appeared at Shelsley in 1921 while still a Cambridge undergraduate, driving a stripped two-seater Hillman named *Quicksilver*. The car was immaculately turned out, and carefully tuned with the help of a fellow undergraduate, Amherst Villiers. The following year Mays returned with a Brescia Bugatti, but was slowed by the remains of a fly which became lodged in his forward carburettor.

In 1923 his little Bugatti, running on the same RD2 alcohol fuel that Ricardo had developed for the TT Vauxhalls, won its class with a startling 52.6 seconds, just 0.4sec shy of the hill record. Then, in the team event at the end of the afternoon, he improved to an astonishing 51.9 seconds. Once again it was not officially deemed a record as it

ABOVE: Eddie Hall's Brescia Bugatti crosses the finish line to record 60.8sec in 1922.

RIGHT: Passing the refreshment tent on the top straight in 1923 is Arthur Waite's 20hp Austin, which won on formula with 77.0sec.

was Mays' second run of the day, but everyone – including several of the magazine reports – accepted it as such. In any case, Mays' earlier run gave him BTD by 0.1 sec from Park's twin-cam works TT Vauxhall. Once again skill and a nimble car were shown to be more effective than mere horsepower: Malcolm Campbell, on his first visit to the hill, won the over-3-litre class with a 4.9-litre Sunbeam, but could not better 54.8sec.

For 1924 Mays, determined to get the record officially this time, arrived with two Brescia Bugattis – you could get two climbs to count if you drove two cars! One was brand new, and the other, the previous year's car, had been updated by the Molsheim factory. The ever-persuasive Mays had got some innovative sponsorship in liquid form from a French drinks firm, and the two cars were called *Cordon Rouge* (a brand of champagne) and *Cordon Bleu* (brandy).

An innovation at this meeting was electrical timing, using equipment loaned by Ferodo: a pneumatic tube ran across the road at both start and finish which identified when a car's wheels crossed it. Cars were still timed by hand as well,

as an insurance against failure of the new technology. Although all times were given to the nearest fifth of a second as usual, the electrical device was apparently able to time to hundredths of a second, because Mays was given 50.82 seconds for his climb in the first Bugatti, and 50.83 in the other. But it wasn't enough. Cyril Paul, driving a much drilled and lightened 2-litre Beardmore, conclusively set a new hill record with a brilliantly smooth and tidy 50.5sec. Mays' two climbs gave him second and third overall, ahead of Eddie Hall in the famous and much-raced Aston Martin *Bunny* and Humphrey Cook's TT Vauxhall.

Before the next Shelsley meeting an accident at another hill changed the shape of British hillclimbing for ever, and actually made Shelsley's position as the country's premier event of its type all the stronger. While motor racing was banned on public roads in Great Britain (unlike in mainland Europe, Northern Ireland and the Isle of Man), sprints and hillclimbs were allowed on the highway, once a permit had been obtained from the RAC. A lot of these events were now being held up and down the country and, as

Matt Park's TT Vauxhall was beaten to BTD in 1923 by Raymond Mays' Bugatti.

Raymond Mays and Amherst Villiers pose in Cordon Bleu at Shelsley in 1924. Standing behind is Mays' faithful mechanic Harold Ayliffe, who worked so hard on the two Bugattis' immaculate preparation.

access could usually not be controlled, spectating tended to be free. Large crowds gathered, and frequently it was impossible to restrain them: they could wander across the road and watch from dangerous vantage points. In 1924 a member of the public who was injured by a competing car sued for damages, and won: the court did not accept the driver's defence that the spectator had accepted the risk by attending the meeting.

Over the winter Raymond Mays had sold both his Bugattis. *Cordon Bleu* went to a fair-haired

Oxford undergraduate called Francis Giveen, and Mays invited him to the family home at Bourne, Eastgate House, to give him some tuition in how to get the best out of it. After some fast runs around the Lincolnshire lanes, with Mays driving and Giveen in the passenger seat, Giveen had a go – and managed to turn the car over. The young man was unhurt and the car only slightly dented, so he entered it for the Essex MC's 28 March event on the very fast Kop Hill course. A dense crowd lined the hill, and it was a miracle when a motorcyclist crashed and injured no-one but himself. Shortly afterwards Giveen lost control of the Bugatti, mounted a bank and broke a spectator's leg. The spectator, a Vauxhall worker from the Luton factory, had apparently refused to move back when asked to do so by a club official. Giveen regained the road and continued his run, driving flat out to the top of the hill. At that point the RAC steward, realising that a really serious accident was waiting to happen, stopped the meeting.

Five days later the RAC Competitions Committee met and decided to withhold all future permits for speed events on public roads – although contests on promenades (like the Brighton Speed Trials) and beaches would be allowed to continue. This left the few events on private land, like Shelsley Walsh, in a strong position. But the RAC also announced that permits for these would only be given if proper arrangements were made for protecting and controlling the public.

Reacting to this, for the 1925 meeting the Midland AC closed the left-hand side of the hill to spectators, and expended a lot of effort in making the right-hand side a superb viewing area. Trees were felled and steps cut in the earth bank to accommodate what one reporter described as "a sloping wall of cheerful faces against a background of flecks of colour of clothing and vegetation" – which is pretty much how the Esses banks look during a Shelsley meeting today. If anything, the changes enhanced the now-traditional Shelsley atmosphere. *The Autocar* spoke of "picnic parties of every description, from the man who was content with a twopenny banana to the party of six who provided a bottle of whisky, a bottle of brandy and siphons of soda for their refreshment".

Henry Segrave took BTD in 1925, handling his Grand Prix Sunbeam with panache.

A MATTER OF TIME

Today, when BTDs can be won or lost by one-hundredth of a second, electronics and computer technology make the accurate recording of times a workaday matter. So it is sobering to remember that, until the mid-1930s, climbs at Shelsley were recorded on a stop-watch accurate to just a fifth of a second. In 1924 the new Ferodo system was used, and Raymond Mays, running his two Brescia Bugattis, was given a time of 50.82 in one and 50.83 in the other. But the RAC would not accept the apparatus as foolproof, and Shelsley reverted to hand-timing on stop watches. Initially the timekeeper was at the top of the hill, listening by telephone to an assistant at the start who shouted "go" when the car was flagged off at the bottom, and stopping his watch when he saw it cross the finish line. This meant that the variable reactions of two people could cumulatively affect the recorded time, which was probably only really accurate to the nearest second at best. The temporary telephone lines, which sometimes gave trouble in bad weather, were not replaced by permanent lines until the 1930s.

Things improved in the 1920s under the disciplined direction of chief timekeeper Major (later Major-General) A.H. Loughborough. He would stand at the start line, holding the flag and shouting into a field telephone which was strapped to his chest and connected to the man with the watches at the top of the hill. Loughborough would shout at one-second intervals "five, four, three, two, one" (the driver straining to read his lips) and then drop the flag.

In 1932 Loughborough replaced this with an ingenious system with five red lights, numbered from 5 down to 1 and each accompanied by an audible "pip", followed by a green light. The time of each climb started from that signal – unlike today, when the green light signifies that a competitor is cleared to start in his own time. To deal with jump-starts, by 1936 a "hockey stick" switch was placed under the car's wheel and, if it moved before the green light, a red light came on 30 yards up the road. The competitor who had jumped the start could stop, reverse, and start again. One false start per competitor was permitted.

In 1936 Loughborough and his assistant Keith Hayes developed the Loughborough-Hayes

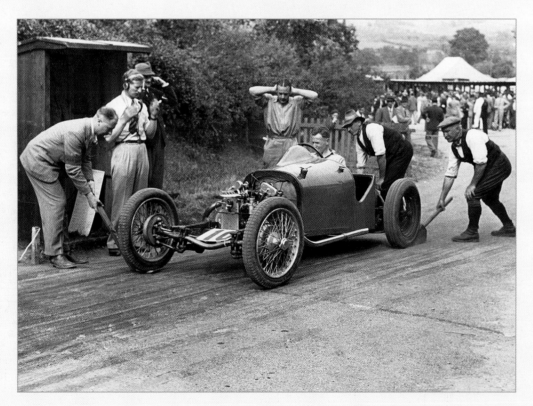

Timing, 1937 style, as Rupert Instone brings the GN Martyr to the line. The hockey stick is under the right front wheel, a chock at the back prevents the car from rolling back, and the timekeeper is in telephone contact with the timing but at the top of the hill.

chronograph, which was very sophisticated for its day. This measured to one-hundredth of a second, and printed out each competitor's times automatically on a pre-prepared card. At first, the moment a car crossed the finish line had been logged by a pneumatic tube across the road, but this was replaced by a strip contact, and ultimately by a light beam. With the advent of a light beam at the bottom of the hill as well, a driver could start in his own time, and jumped starts became a thing of the past. In the late 1960s came the Burt strut, devised by Ron Smith for Patsy Burt's record-breaking attempts. This was a simple piece of black metal mounted vertically on the front of the car, to cut the light beam cleanly. It is now mandatory for all hillclimb cars.

Electronics soon made digital clocks possible, large enough to be seen by spectators, with a speed trap just before the braking area into the Esses and another at the finish line. Another was introduced at the start line to indicate the time taken by each car to cover the first 64 feet, and thus show who

had used the start well and who hadn't.

Today, of course, serious hillclimbers incorporate data-logging on their cars which will capture every detail of gear-change points, engine revs, braking efficiency and so on for down-loading and study at the bottom of the hill. Jonathan Toulmin was one of the first to try this on his Lola-Rover as early as 1990.

Maurice Harvey's front-drive Alvis tied for second BTD in 1925.

Star attraction in 1925 was the great racer and, later, record-breaker on land and water, Henry O'Neal De Hane Segrave, who had won the 1923 French Grand Prix for Sunbeam. Wearing a smart lounge suit, and on a surface wet from the heavy thunderstorm that briefly halted the meeting, he handled his 2-litre Grand Prix Sunbeam with elegant smoothness to take BTD in 53.8sec, a very impressive performance on his first visit to Shelsley. He would have examined the course on foot in the morning, for a new rule required every competitor, old and new, to sign a chit saying he or she had walked the hill. There was a tie for second BTD between C.M. Harvey in the stripped works front-wheel-drive Alvis and the supercharged 2-litre Mercedes of E.A. Meyner. Raymond Mays, having an unsuccessful foray that

year with a supercharged 1500cc AC single-seater, was somewhat slower.

Until now there had only been one Shelsley Walsh hillclimb each year, apart from an impromptu closed-to-club event in September 1909 (which is ignored by most of the record books, and was won "on formula" by C.J. Newey's de Dion). But in July 1926 a second event was introduced for amateurs, defined as "those who are not connected with, or do not receive remuneration from, the automobile or allied trades". Eddie Hall's touring Vauxhall 30/98 had set fastest time when the heavens opened to release torrential rain. The meeting was suspended, resumed and then abandoned, with the racing car classes postponed to the main meeting in September.

Which meant that one of the first to ascend two months later was Basil Davenport in his 1500cc GN-based, home-brewed machine, *Spider*. It was the fastest ever: 48.8 seconds. Davenport, having terrorised most of the north-country hillclimb and sprint venues, first ventured south to Shelsley in 1924 and soon made it his adopted home.

In 1925 he'd been only 0.8sec off Segrave's time, even though the V-twin seized on the final straight, leaving him to coast over the line with a dead engine. That record climb in 1926 was historic in many ways: it was the first under 50 seconds, it took a huge 1.7sec off the old record, and it was the first BTD by a genus that would become known as the Shelsley Special – a minimalist car built from assorted parts, usually by an amateur enthusiast, for no other purpose than to ascend this Worcestershire hill, and others like it, as rapidly as possible.

Davenport, like Mays, would continue to leave his stamp on Shelsley for many years to come. He was unbeaten at every Shelsley for the next three years, and was still competing in variations of his original car more than 40 years later.

Davenport achieved consecutive BTDs at the next five meetings, progressively lowering the record in one-second chunks, from 48.8 to 47.8 (September 1927) and 46.8 (May 1928). By now a marvellous Shelsley rivalry had developed between Davenport and Mays, outlined in sharp relief by the difference of character in both man and car.

Davenport, the gruff, no-nonsense North Country mill owner, liked to compete wearing an old brown cow gown, fastened around his waist with a length of baler twine. His car was developed over each winter to be ever more powerful and ever lighter, but deliberately no effort was expended on its appearance. As a result *Spider* was so scruffy that, arriving for the May 1926 meeting, the record holder was initially refused entrance to the paddock because the policeman on the gate could not believe he was a competitor.

Raymond Mays was an elegant, debonair young man who, during the week, liked nothing more than to travel from his Lincolnshire home to London's West End to see a musical show by his

Raymond Mays with Peter Berthon in Harold Clay's TT Vauxhall in September 1926. By 1928 he had a Vauxhall of his own, which developed into the Villiers Supercharge.

friend Ivor Novello. His cars and his clothes were always immaculate – he was known to put each foot in turn on a box so that his mechanic could polish his shoes. Mays' driving was equally smooth and stylish, his face invariably wearing a fixed grin of concentration under the beret he wore to keep his thinning hair in place. And he was a hugely determined competitor. For the September 1926 meeting he borrowed Harold Clay's scarlet TT Vauxhall and was just 0.6sec slower than Davenport. For 1927 he was campaigning a works-supported 2-litre supercharged Targa Florio Mercedes, but in July he could only make equal second fastest. This was the first meeting when every competitor got two runs, with the faster one to count, and the slower one only taken into account to decide dead heats.

The September meeting that year started out

Doris Wilson, Leslie's sister, shouldered the role of secretary of the meeting.

as the wettest yet. After Sammy Davis had made an Ascent of Honour in a 3-litre Bentley, like the one with which he and Dr J.D. Benjafield had sensationally won the Le Mans 24 Hours two months earlier, the hill was still slippery when Davenport set his second record. Mays improved to a stirring 48.2sec to take second. The imperturbable Basil preferred the hill to be slightly damp, as he found it bound the loose surface together better.

Mays decided to buy Humphrey Cook's TT Vauxhall – it cost him £275 – and spent the winter of 1927 developing it, with the help of Amherst Villiers, into the famous supercharged Vauxhall Villiers. But Davenport was busy too, and his careful development work included brewing his own alcohol fuel in a disused henhouse. The Vauxhall Villiers was barely ready for the May 1928 event: it was immaculately turned out, of course, in Mays' favourite shade of pale blue-grey, with the dapper Mays accompanied by his now customary passenger, a young RAF pilot called Peter Berthon – who went on to design both the ERA and the BRM. But the Vauxhall's engine failed soon after the start line, so Davenport's 46.8sec record climb was easily fastest. In July Spider found another three-fifths to achieve 46.2sec, beating the now healthy Vauxhall Villiers by all of 1.8sec.

If proof were needed of the stature to which Shelsley Walsh had risen, that July 1928 meeting provided it, for the huge crowd of spectators included the Prime Minister, Stanley Baldwin, who watched the action from the members' enclosure at the Esses. The thought of Tony Blair, surrounded by a posse of security men, spending an afternoon in 2005 enjoying a round of the British Hillclimb Championship stretches the imagination somewhat. Once more the hill was opened by a Climb of Honour, Woolf Barnato commemorating his Le Mans victory with a four-and-a-half Bentley. The idea of demonstration climbs at Shelsley by significant cars and great drivers was a happy one, and became a tradition that continues to this day.

A public address system had been installed for the first time, and already it was helping to build the atmosphere of Shelsley, as *The Motor* described:

The loudspeaker spoke: "B.H. Davenport is about to leave the start." A tense hush

descended on the crowd, and then from far below through the trees came a rapid crescendo of noise that made spectators hold their breaths and crane eagerly forward. With a terrific crackle from the two exhaust pipes the shabby-looking little car simply hurtled up to the S-bend. Came a moment's dead silence as the driver cut out and hunched himself to heave the jigging front wheels round the corner. Another roar between the bends, again a moment's silence, and then, flat out, "Spider" simply leapt up the straight to the finish. "B.H. Davenport, driving Frazer Nash No 39, forty-six and one-fifth seconds," said the loudspeakers. One point six clipped off his own record! What an artist.

And now came Raymond Mays on the supercharged Vauxhall-Villiers Special, aptly nicknamed "Voronoff". Could he beat Davenport? That's what the crowd were asking. With the record at 47.8 he had a chance, said the experts, but at 46.2 – no! They were dead right, for Mays, though he gave of his best – and he can drive – could only manage 48 seconds. It was a magnificent climb, too.

While the battle for BTD waged between Basil Davenport and Raymond Mays tended to be the climax of each meeting, the atmosphere of Shelsley continued to be enriched by the fascinating variety of cars and drivers in the rest of the entry. Every class, from the smallest production light cars to hefty dignified tourers, was always hotly contested. The programme usually encompassed three segments – sports and standard touring cars,

At the end of the 1924 meeting, the crowds walk back down the hill. By now Shelsley Walsh was a national institution.

Jammed traffic waiting to leave the car park in 1924. All sorts came to Shelsley: in the queue are Austin 7, Morris Cowley and Ford Model T as well as grander limousines with chauffeurs.

unlimited racing cars, and a team event, for which clubs put forward three representatives. Meanwhile the "Formula" handicap system, calculated to take into account the weight of the car and its horsepower or, from 1924, its engine capacity, continued until 1929, when the final winner on handicap was Derek Burcher's Riley Nine. There were regulars who came near to BTD glory but never quite made it, like the very smooth E.L.F Mucklow, whose red GN was named *Tiger Tim* after a children's comic character of the day, and whose best was joint second BTD with Mays in 1926. And there were the wilder souls, whose hairier moments were recounted with glee by the motoring press:

> *F.B. Taylor is lucky to be alive. In his straight-eight Bugatti he came round the lower curve (Kennel) very fast in a skid, shot up the straight*

and endeavoured to get round the easier curve (Crossing) at too fast a pace. Thereafter he became the plaything of natural forces. Still hurtling forward, the car ran up the right-hand bank with its right wheels, and lay over until the left-hand hubcaps touched the road; gravity took Taylor like a sack and flung him out of his seat onto the passenger seat, and his head and shoulders scraped within an inch of the road. Then, for no obvious reason, the car came down off the bank, still shifting fast, still over on its side, and righted onto its four wheels. A dazed Taylor, still clutching the wheel with one hand, hauled himself back somehow and dashed on again...

As Norman Coates on the supercharged Arab got to the first sharp left-hand bend he pulled his off-side front tyre off the rim. The tube exuded, unpunctured, with a rapidly-growing balloon at its weakest point. The loose cover made steering difficult and there were shouts of excitement and alarm as the car plunged, skidding wildly, from side to side. The tube, with its ridiculous bulge, came out more and more, swinging round and round like a flail and causing the car to swerve, zigzagging up the hill, watched by a thrilled but anxious crowd. At length the tube burst, but the driver reached the top without mishap.

Davenport beat Mays again in the first meeting of 1929. Little winter work had been done on the Vauxhall Villiers, because Amherst Villiers was busy with his work supercharging the Tim Birkin/Dorothy Paget Bentleys. But after this latest defeat a major engine rebuild was put in hand in search of 250bhp. More horses brought more wheelspin, so Villiers hit on the novel idea of doubling up the rear wheels, as on a heavy lorry. A pair of special twin wire wheels was made up,

just in time for the September meeting. It was an idea that would be much copied.

For the first time competitors were allowed to practise on the previous day, a Friday, which must have helped Earl Howe, who was making his Shelsley debut. He had bought the huge works 7.1-litre supercharged Mercedes SSK with which Caracciola had won the TT four weeks earlier, and got this daunting car up the hill in a remarkable 47.6sec, good enough for third BTD. But the real battle, once again, was between Davenport and Mays.

An era was about to end, and another begin. *Spider* did a 47 dead on its first run, 0.8sec off its best, but Mays, with Berthon beside him as usual, was on top form and set a new record at 46 dead. Davenport came to the line to reply, but almost at once *Spider*'s engine cried enough. Mays, with the pressure off, was able to go even quicker, posting a brilliant 45.6sec. It was the first of five Shelsley records for him. Twenty years later, he would still be setting Best Time of Day.

Having arrived in this magnificent road-going Mercedes, Earl Howe donned leather helmet and overalls to set third BTD in his new ex-works SSK racer, September 1929.

SHELSLEY WALSH GROWS UP 1930–1939

As the 1920s gave way to the 1930s, Shelsley Walsh was changing too. The spidery motorcycle-engined lightweight specials, which had ruled for most of the past decade, were now threatened by more costly, sophisticated machinery that could win races on the tracks of Europe, but still be quick within the hill's peculiarly demanding confines. But the Shelsley Specials would fight back, become more advanced themselves, and have their day again.

Fittingly, the new decade was ushered in by Shelsley's most international event yet. The European Hillclimb Championship boasted ten rounds across the continent, including great mountain venues like Klausen in Switzerland, Freiburg in Germany and Mont Ventoux in France. In 1930, for the first time, a British round was added, and Shelsley Walsh was the obvious choice of venue. For the first time the loose, dusty gravel surface was properly sealed from bottom to top, the hill being described by *The Autocar* as "now grouted with small flints, sprayed with bitumen and water, and rolled".

The entry included Europe's acknowledged master of hillclimbing, the Austrian-born Hans Stuck von Villiez, and his blue and white 3-litre Austro-Daimler. By then he only needed a class victory to put that year's championship title more or less in his pocket. Running in the sports car class was the famous road racer Rudi Caracciola, in a fully road-equipped 7.1-litre 38/220 SSK Mercedes.

Mays' elderly Vauxhall had been completely rebuilt over the winter, and was now called the Villiers Supercharge. It was appreciably lower, with a square, squat radiator and a big tube-shaped intercooler on the side of the bonnet to cool the mixture coming from the supercharger on its way to the inlet manifold – typical of the effort that Mays and Amherst Villiers were putting into the car in their quest for the record. Horsepower was now approaching 300bhp, but the heavy supercharger, and the steel plates strengthening the cracked old chassis, brought the weight almost to 30cwt. Feverish work saw the car still being bolted together in the early hours of the Saturday of the event. Mays decided on a trial run by driving it from Bourne to Shelsley, but the car broke down. Having abandoned it in a Lincolnshire lockup, the team drove on in Mays' Lagonda to spectate.

Mays' non-start left Davenport even more determined that his rude device should take the fight to the foreign visitors. His first effort – aided no doubt by the new surface – was a startling 44.6sec, enough to break Mays' hill record by a clear second. Then Stuck attacked the hill, with such smoothness and polish that he looked almost slow. His time was 42.8sec, almost three seconds below the record. To underline his superiority and consistency, the time for his second run was identical. It was a record that was to stand for three years. Meanwhile, Caracciola's big car set a new sports car record in 46.8sec, with the young but already bulky Alfred Neubauer, who went on to become one of the best Grand Prix team managers in history, in the passenger seat.

The Villiers Supercharge was finally on song for

Unforgettable sight: Hans Stuck grappling with the Grand Prix Auto Union on a narrow, bumpy, wet Shelsley on 6 June 1936.

ABOVE: Hillclimb specialist Hans Stuck brought superb style and polish to his July 1930 BTD in the works Austro-Daimler.

RIGHT: The great Rudi Caracciola has a quick cigarette before tackling the hill in the big SSK Mercedes.

the September "amateur" meeting. It rained that day, so Mays' BTD in slithery conditions was impressive at 46.4sec. Dick Nash, in the ex-Archie Frazer-Nash supercharged *Terror*, was the only other runner to better 50sec with a 48.8. His day was to come just nine months later, when the July 1931 meeting was again a round of the European Hillclimb Championship. Once again Caracciola and Stuck were expected, as well as several more of the continental contenders, including Louis Chiron with a Bugatti (an unlikely entry, with the Belgian GP at Spa on the same weekend). As it turned out, none of them appeared. *The Motor* explained with disdain:

> *There was to have been a whole host of foreign drivers, but a bare fortnight before the event they constituted themselves into a sort of unofficial Trades Union and all stood out for their expenses. The Midland Automobile Club*

quite rightly stuck to their rule to offer
hospitality, but not to pay expenses of foreign
competitors. If they wanted to score more points
in the European Mountain Championship, why
should the drivers not pay for the privilege?

However, there was some overseas participation.
Two works entries were received from the Spanish
Nacional Pescara firm, and two Chevrolet trucks
with the cars, drivers and mechanics on board set
out from Barcelona for the long drive north. Leslie
Wilson had heard that the only address they knew
was "Shelsley Walsh, England", and that none of
them spoke English, so he wasn't surprised when
Friday practice came and went, and there was no
sign of them. But in the early hours of Saturday
morning, the trucks rolled into the Shelsley
paddock, and disgorged two yellow racers with
twin-cam straight-eight 3-litre engines. As they
missed practice and had never seen the hill before,

or anything like it, their drivers – jolly, round-faced
Juan Zanelli and serious-looking Esteban Tort –
were allowed trial runs on Saturday morning. At
once they found their cars seriously over-geared
for the short hill, and the tired mechanics set
about changing ratios. During the afternoon they
put on an excellent display, climbing in 44.4sec and
45.6sec, and earned the applause of the crowd.

Davenport's 46.2 was well off *Spider*'s best.
Noel Carr turned in a hectic 44.0 in his Bugatti,
having straightened the car out overnight after a
practice shunt. Raymond Mays managed a fiery
43.6sec in the Villiers. But Dick Nash, grim-faced
under his crash helmet, was the man that day,
brave and clean with *Terror*. He beat Mays' time
by a fifth of a second to take his first BTD – and
become, at that point, the fastest Englishman up
Shelsley, winning the Shelsley International Cup
and the not inconsiderable sum of 100 guineas.
Years later, John Bolster described Nash as "shy,

*Caracciola's passenger in
the works Mercedes in
July 1930 was future
Grand Prix team
manager Alfred
Neubauer.*

Dick Nash lifts a wheel approaching the Top Ess on his July 1931 BTD run in the Frazer Nash Terror. Note the twin rear wheels.

quiet, almost diffident, but once in a car his whole nature seemed to change, and ferocious would not be too strong a word to describe his handling of his supercharged projectile". However, Mays was back on top at the wet September meeting, beating Nash by 2.4sec. Almost unnoticed in a Riley Brooklands Nine was one R.J. Beattie-Seaman, who climbed in a tardy 78.4sec. In his first speed event, 18-year-old Dick Seaman showed little of the talent that would make him a Grand Prix winner for Mercedes-Benz before his death at Spa in 1939.

With Shelsley's status in the motorsport world continuing to grow, the ambitious Midland Automobile Club now announced plans to extend the hill by a further 400 yards. A hairpin after the finish line would take cars back parallel to the final straight to make a total distance of 1400 yards. But, after almost a year of discussion, the voices pleading for Shelsley to remain at its already classic distance prevailed, and the project was dropped.

The major drama of the June 1932 meeting took place in practice. Lord Howe had heard about Ettore Bugatti's new four-wheel-drive 4.9-litre Type 53 racing car, and made a personal approach to the great man to persuade him to send it to Shelsley for its competition debut. The car duly arrived in Worcestershire with a team of works mechanics, and Ettore's son Jean to drive it. During Friday practice, rumour began to spread of the car's extraordinary speed – "its getaway was unbelievably rapid" said one onlooker, "resembling nothing so much as an object suddenly released when tied to a tightly stretched piece of elastic". Leslie Wilson professed himself privately astonished by the car's times, but he steadfastly refused to release them, and never confirmed the generally-held view that on his second practice run Jean Bugatti had unofficially broken the hill record.

We will never know whether it might have done so officially, for the visitor was allowed the courtesy of a third practice run, and soon after the start the big blue Bugatti got out of shape. As

Jean Bugatti fought with the car it hit the bank hard at Kennel and was damaged beyond immediate repair.

Lord Howe prevailed upon the mortified Jean to telephone his father from Leslie Wilson's hut and break the news. "Holding the receiver in one hand, young Bugatti gesticulated wildly with the other while he poured a flood of voluble French into the mouthpiece, becoming more and more excited as the conversation progressed…" On the Saturday Jean was allowed to drive instead the lovely red and black Type 55 road car in which he had arrived. His time was faster than all the others in his class but, as he was not entered, he could not qualify for an award. Hastily a special cup was found for him, so that after his fraught weekend he would not return to Molsheim empty-handed.

The above version of the Jean Bugatti incident is as it was reported in the magazines of the day. However, more recent Shelsley historians have cast doubt on whether he set those astonishing practice times at all, believing that the story of the two rapid practice runs may have been concocted by Howe and Wilson to mollify Ettore Bugatti. Certainly the Type 53 was troubled by a misfire in the paddock on Friday morning, and it may well be that the accident happened on Jean's first and only run.

Anyway, Bugatti honour was satisfied, because a surprise BTD came from Earl Howe in his own 2.3-litre Type 51, with which he'd finished fourth in the Monaco Grand Prix two months before. He climbed in 44.0sec on his first run, 0.6sec faster than Mays in the Villiers Supercharge. *Terror* stopped on its first run, and Dick Nash spoiled its second by ricocheting off both banks out of the Esses. And then it rained.

Although still billed as the "amateur" Shelsley, the September meeting was now open to all comers. The Villiers was sidelined when the crank broke while Raymond Mays was warming it up on the public road between Shelsley and Martley, although he did set a new sports car record with his much-modified and lightened Invicta. Nevertheless there was a wonderful battle for BTD between Dick Nash in *Terror* and Noel Carr's always furiously driven Bugatti.

On his first run Nash did 44.4sec, and Carr replied with 43.6. For his second attempt Nash got down to a brilliant 43.2, so now it was all down to the spectacular Noel Carr. But the red Bugatti arrived far too fast at the Esses and climbed the bank. Carr's effort at BTD was over – as far as he was concerned, however, his day's motorsport wasn't. He kept the engine running as the car was manhandled down the bank by the marshals, and as soon as it was back on the tarmac he roared away again at once, scattering the marshals as he went. Unfortunately the breakdown truck had

June 1932: the young Jean Bugatti grins in anticipation of taking the four-wheel-drive Type 53 up the hill. But his practice run ended in disaster.

With the Type 53 wrecked, Jean Bugatti had to make do with a road-going Type 55 on the Saturday.

already been summoned down from the top of the hill to rescue his car, and was making its ponderous way towards the Top Ess just as Carr came out of it. It was just as well that they met where the steep banks gave way to grass verges. Carr kept his foot hard down, and somehow the Bugatti squeezed through the gap, making it to the finish without further incident. But Dick Nash had his second BTD.

The May 1933 meeting was wet again. Mays took another BTD with the Villiers on 44.8. Dick Nash had replaced *Terror* with a new Frazer-Nash-based car, *The Spook*, which he took to second BTD on 45.6sec, but an exciting runner was the ex-Birkin 2.5-litre Maserati 8C in the hands of a Cambridge undergraduate, a wealthy young American called Whitney Straight. After having his first time disallowed because of a false start, he managed 47.8sec when the rain was at its worst. Straight also ran his mighty Bentley 8-litre saloon in the sports car class. Count Gigi Premoli had spent four days towing his supercharged Maserati-powered Bugatti hybrid all the way from Milan and was rewarded with a class win, while John Bolster's tiny V-twin-powered, wooden-chassis Shelsley Special, *Bloody Mary*, performed a dramatic roll at the Esses, with the driver's bare head banging along the tarmac as the car went over. Bolster was extricated from the wreckage and carried off for medical attention, calling out from the stretcher: "Is Mary's petrol turned off?"

Hans Stuck's record had now stood for three years, but the September 1933 meeting was one of those events when the record books get rewritten. As well as the faithful Villiers, Raymond Mays brought his exciting new project: the White Riley. With Murray Jamieson and Peter Berthon, he had built up a light 1500cc supercharged car using factory-loaned Riley parts. On the test-bed, went the gossip, the engine had run at an unprecedented 8000rpm. On its first climb the

elegant little car recorded a 42.2sec, and once again Mays held the Shelsley record.

But only for a matter of minutes. Straight slid aboard the big black Maserati and produced the first-ever sub-42 climb with a 41.4sec. In the Villiers Mays posted 42.4, still better than Stuck's old record, and his best-ever in the old car, which was appearing in his hands for the last time. Then Straight had his second climb in the Maserati and found another fifth of a second, leaving the record at a marvellous 41.2sec.

It was altogether a vintage Shelsley. The new records were witnessed by a record 16,000 spectators and, with the field limited to 70 starters, many hopeful entrants had to be turned away. To speed up the programme and improve its quality, a rule was now being imposed under which any runner whose first time was longer than 60sec did not qualify for a second run. Bolster had straightened out *Bloody Mary*, and fought her up the hill to a 45.8sec class win, but less successful

Some recompense for Bugatti's faux pas at the June 1932 meeting was Earl Howe's BTD with his own Type 51.

was a young man listed in the programme as J. Justice, who left the start in a twin JAP-engined special but failed to get to the Esses. He later found more fulfilment as the respected bearded actor James Robertson Justice. Cynthia Sedgwick broke Mrs "Bill" Wisdom's ladies' record with her Frazer Nash, but she didn't hold it long. At the following meeting Barbara Skinner, of the SU (Skinners Union) carburettor family and soon to become Mrs John Bolster, took it with her blown Morris Minor Special.

As for Whitney Straight, he had cut short his studies at Cambridge to become a full-time racing driver and leader of his own team, with bases in London and Milan, and had bought no fewer than three new 2.9-litre 8CM Grand Prix cars from the Maserati factory. He brought one to the June 1934 meeting, painted in the American racing colours of blue and white. The car arrived without twin rear wheels, and in practice Straight was unhappy with its handling, so he had twin rears flown in

A fine shot of Count Gigi Premoli's hybrid Maserati-Bugatti winning its class at the May 1933 meeting.

to Worcestershire by light aircraft. Thus equipped, he took the powerful Maserati off the line in second gear, changing directly into top before Kennel. It was a devastating climb: 40 seconds dead, and 1.2 seconds off his own record.

The car magazines had been full of Raymond Mays' new creation, the ERA, backed by Humphrey Cook and developed by Peter Berthon on a Reid Railton-designed chassis, with Murray Jamieson breathing on the supercharged Riley-based engine. But it wasn't ready, and Mays brought the White Riley instead. After one run disallowed because of a jumped start, he posted 42.8sec – a long way off Straight, but still second BTD. Tom Fotheringham set a surprise third best BTD with his 2.3-litre Bugatti on 43.0, while Eddie Hall, a hugely experienced Shelsley stalwart for many years with Bugatti, Aston Martin, Vauxhall, Arrol Aster and Bentley cars, broke the sports car record in his blown MG K3 Magnette with a remarkable 43.2sec. Bolster's *Bloody Mary* now

had not one but two V-twin engines, and thus was running in the 2-litre racing car class. Darting from side to side, with the tall, moustachioed driver, elbows akimbo, working hard in the impossibly cramped cockpit, it won the class in 44.2sec.

The ERA was at last ready for the September meeting, and Mays entered two, the original 1500cc R1, which had already been raced, and a brand-new 2-litre, R3. The 1500 was brought to Shelsley by van, but the 2-litre, which had barely turned a wheel, was fitted with makeshift plywood mudguards and trade plates, and Mays nonchalantly drove it on the public roads from Lincolnshire to Shelsley. An ERA on the road, going by Mays' own description, must have been quite a sight:

The exhilaration of that ride can scarcely be conveyed in words. A touch of the throttle made ordinary main road hills feel like downgrades, and when I really trod on things the ERA rocketed to 100mph on steep hills in an incredibly short time. Yet through towns and villages she would potter quietly along on a mere whiff of throttle.

For the event it rained again, but Mays made the best of the conditions to clock 44.0 in the 2-litre. Whitney Straight, his Maserati back to his favourite black and silver colours, got close but not close enough – a fifth of a second slower. It was his last appearance at Shelsley. The following year he announced his retirement from racing, both to

Taking a tight line at the Top Ess, Whitney Straight carves a huge 1.6 seconds off the hill record with the supercharged Maserati, September 1933.

65

Raymond Mays' "White Riley" was the precursor of the ERA. For just a few minutes in September 1933 it held the hill record.

allow him to concentrate on his business career – he went on to become chairman of BOAC and vice-chairman of Rolls-Royce – and because of his forthcoming marriage.

Until now Leslie Wilson had combined his duties as MAC secretary with managing his Birmingham garage business, Economical Cars Ltd. But Shelsley's growth meant that the club was now able to employ him full-time. The garage was closed and Leslie moved into new offices at 87 Edmund Street, with as full-time secretary the delightfully-named Miss Marjorie Barnacle, who had been helping out since leaving school.

Meanwhile, with Straight's record on exactly 40 seconds, the goal of a sub-40secs time at Shelsley, once thought to be physically impossible, was beckoning. Fittingly it happened at the 30th anniversary meeting, in May 1935, and it happened twice – one man, one marque, two cars. First Raymond Mays went up in the little 1500cc ERA in 39.8sec and then, minutes later, he went even faster with the 2-litre to leave the record at 39.6sec. Another great achievement came from Pat Driscoll's supercharged single-seater Austin 7, with 43.4sec. This was faster than a whole raft of more exotic machinery, like Chris Staniland's Grand Prix Type 51 Bugatti and Dick Shuttleworth's P3 Alfa Romeo.

Regulations governing which cars could run in the sports car class were tightened up for this meeting: they had to be in full touring trim, with lights and wings. The best of them was a Frazer Nash driven by a well-to-do young man of Anglo-Indian extraction, educated at Harrow and Clare College, Cambridge, called Alfred Fane Peers Agabeg. He'd first appeared at Shelsley in a Frazer Nash in 1932: already he had dropped his awkward surname and called himself A.F.P. Fane, and signed his name Fane Fane. At a time when ex-public school chaps tended to address each other by their surnames, he became plain "Fane" to everyone.

That day Sir Malcolm Campbell made his first visit to Shelsley for a decade, demonstrating and then competing in the ex-Segrave 4-litre V12 Sunbeam and posting a doughty 44.4sec in this big old car. Doreen Evans, in the single-seater R-type MG, took a worthy 1.2sec out of Barbara Skinner's ladies' record with 45.4sec.

And it was the battle for the ladies' record that played the starring role in the September meeting.

ABOVE: Shelsley heroes: (from left) Mays, Straight and Howe in June 1934 after Straight reduced the record to 40 seconds dead.

BELOW: Eddie Hall's blown MG Magnette set a new sports car record in June 1934 at 43.2sec.

irrepressible Leslie Wilson persuaded Auto Union to send a car to the June meeting for Hans Stuck. Stuck had been competing in European mountain hillclimbs with a specially-built short-wheelbase 5.3-litre version of the latest supercharged V16 Grand Prix car, complete with twinned rear wheels. It was rather like Jean Todt and Ross Brawn having a current F1 Ferrari modified for hillclimbing, and sending it to Worcestershire for Michael Schumacher to drive.

Stuck, of course, had held the hill record for three years after his previous visit in 1930 and, although the Auto Union's 550bhp would make it a huge handful for the short, sharp Shelsley dash, he was strongly tipped to take it again. There were one or two murmurs of disapproval during Friday practice when the tall, aristocratic Stuck and his sensational silver projectile, with its long, louvred tail sprouting sixteen shrieking stub exhausts, were allowed rather more practice runs than anyone else. But it was generally, if unofficially, agreed that his best practice time was 39.6sec, equalling Mays' record. Mays, on the other hand, had run into trouble with the 2-litre ERA, which blew its engine in practice. He now had only the 1500cc car at his disposal. But on Saturday his luck changed: it rained.

The rain was just beginning as Mays did his first run in the little ERA, taking a conservative 41.6sec. But for both of Stuck's runs the track was well and truly wet and greasy, leaving him to fight the big Auto Union up the narrow hill in a succession of fish-tailing, wheel-spinning, opposite-lock slides. His best was only 45.2sec – merely seventh equal BTD with the little MG of Denis Evans. But it was enthralling both to watch and hear, and the sodden crowd loved it, as did *The Motor*'s reporter:

Kay Petre was in the ex-Mays White Riley, and she and Doreen Evans battled all day, ending up after their second runs with a dead-heat. It was resolved by an extra run-off between the two, with Petre leaving the record at a brilliant 43.8. Only five males were quicker that day. On this dry but windy day BTD went again to Mays: driving a new 2-litre ERA, R4B, he equalled but did not beat his own record, and set second BTD in good old R1.

In 1936 perhaps the most dramatic machine ever to compete at Shelsley came to the hill. The

With a great swirl of twin rear tyres the silver projectile shot round Kennel Bend. It seemed gigantic on the narrow road, and there seemed barely a foot to spare between the high banks. Stuck was unable to use anything like full throttle at any time. His foot jabbed the accelerator every time the tail seemed roughly in line with the radiator, the independently-sprung wheels danced and dithered madly, the tail swung with spinning wheels from side to side each time the engine roared, and the acceleration between slides was truly awe-inspiring. He fought the car up the hill with his elbows jerking like a man rowing, wrenching the wheel through half a turn with immense speed. The tail wagged viciously, the engine roared, his arms worked like pumps, and the trees re-echoed the bellowings of the big engine.

Afterwards, Stuck confessed that he'd had to lift off before the top of the hill. "I had to cut out at least 50 metres before the finish. There were some cars in the way in the field at the top. Really, there isn't very much room to pull up." The thought of running out of tarmac and having to rein in an Auto Union on wet grass must have been worrying. However, Stuck good-humouredly maintained that his real problem was merely "too many horsepowers".

In fact, it was a day for the little cars. Equal second, fourth, fifth and sixth fastest times were set – all before the rain came – by the astonishing little single-seater Austin 7s. German Walter Baumer, in a side-valve version, tied for second BTD with Fane's twin-supercharged Frazer-Nash single-seater, with the twin-cam works cars of Charles Goodacre and Charlie Dodson third and fifth, split by A.N.L. Maclachlan's private side-valve.

That September the weather was yet worse, and even Leslie Wilson's normally smooth organisation was thrown out of gear by the torrential rain. Paddock and car parks were ankle deep in mud, problems with the timing gear further delayed things, and in the gathering gloom several cars still had to make their second climb when, at almost 7.30pm, there was a big accident after the finish line. Philip Jucker's single-seater Alta was being driven by May Cunliffe, now Mrs Millington. Somehow she got her foot caught between throttle and brake, and plunged across wet fields

Pre-war the orchard on the right of the hill did duty as the paddock. Today, with the trees gone, it is the public car park.

KEEPING US INFORMED

A public address system was first used at Shelsley in 1928. Originally the idea was simply for an official to announce which car was on the line, so that spectators up the hill knew who was coming, and then read out the times achieved. But Bentley racer and *The Autocar* sports editor S.C.H. "Sammy" Davis was recruited as the first proper commentator, and he was both knowledgeable and possessed of a delightful sense of fun. So very quickly more information was added about the history of driver and car; wit and humour crept in too.

In 1931 the editor of *The Light Car*, Eric Findon, made his first commentary. The operation was primitive:

We were ensconced in a kind of bathing tent in the grounds of the cottage by the start line, separated from the track by three feet of grass and a five-foot hedge, with the microphone hung from a bar at the open end of the tent. It was impossible for me to see the start, so while Mrs Findon glued herself heroically to the telephone so she could tell me the time of each ascent, Miss Findon, ignoring the grave risk of falling

over into the roadway, leaned well into the hedge and shouted out the number of the car that was coming to the line. It was not until a car had breasted the rise beyond the start that I was able to see it, but from that point I endeavoured to describe how it was being driven and so on. Gathering courage as the afternoon proceeded, I endeavoured to introduce a little colour into my description and one or two good-natured leg-pulls.

In 1932 history was made when the BBC came to Shelsley Walsh for the June meeting and broadcast the course commentary in three segments totalling 1 hour 20 minutes. It went out both on the National Programme and the Empire Service, so that live coverage of the event was heard as far away as Australia. One listener in Sri Lanka wrote "we were transported in spirit to Shelsley Walsh, thanks to an excellent broadcast which came over almost perfectly. When Hall's Magnette made its second run we heard that wonderful exhaust note, broken by wheelspin as he got away from the Top 'S'...absolutely marvellous."

RIGHT: The original Vox Villa with (from left) Eric Findon, daughter Jo, wife Kit, Val Valentine and Alan Jensen of Jensen Cars.

FAR RIGHT: The Crossing commentary box in 1951 with Gerry Flewitt at work.

It was the first motorsport event in mainland Britain to be covered on the air. Findon, nicknamed "Vox", had now moved to the passenger seat of a parked Rover Ten on the other side of the start line, with wife and telephone in the back seat writing down times and daughter passing him slips of paper. For the BBC output a second commentator, BBC man Major Vernon Brook, was positioned in a box at the Esses, and after Findon had cast covetous looks at this the MAC eventually built him a proper wooden hut and christened it Vox Villa.

It is there to this day, although it got a sorely needed rebuild in 1971, and is occupied by today's course commentators John Moody and his son Toby. Nowadays there are two more commentary positions, at the Crossing and at the exit to the Esses. As the fastest climbs occupy less than 25 seconds, very quick handovers are required between the three commentators. They include past Jaguar racer Max Trimble, John Roberts, Mark Richardson, Colin Wood, Michael Bowers and former hillclimber Chris Drewett.

Findon went on to commentate for the BBC from the TT at Ards, from Brooklands, Donington and Crystal Palace. At Shelsley, three commentary points were tried for one BBC broadcast, with Vox at the start line, a BBC man at the finish, and none other than Lord Howe at the Esses. Thereafter they reverted to the start and the Esses only, with former racer and later Austin PR and record-breaker Alan Hess at the Esses, and now for the first time the

ABOVE LEFT: Chief commentator and club president John Moody flanked by son Toby (left) and Mark Richardson.

ABOVE RIGHT: More of today's commentary team: Michael Bowers (left) and Max Trimble.

LEFT: Murray Walker makes a guest return to the place where he did his first-ever commentary in 1948.

Esses commentary became part of the public address as well.

Other commentary names down the years have included John Bolster, John Hay and his son Neville, Keith Douglas and his son Russell, and Shelsley historian, reporter and photographer Bob Cooper. Most famous of all Shelsley's past commentators is Murray Walker, who made his first-ever commentary in what was to become more than half a century of motorsport broadcasting on television and radio. His father Graham Walker, a great motorcycle racer and journalist, was unable to do a BBC Shelsley broadcast in 1948, and the Shelsley PA commentator, Charlie Markham, did it instead. Graham suggested his boy could stand in on the PA: the BBC producer happened to hear him, and offered him an audition. The rest is history.

Raymond Mays brings the first ERA, R1, to the line at the September 1935 meeting. Peter Berthon stands beside the car.

and backwards through a barbed wire fence, sustaining various injuries, including a broken jaw. At that point the meeting was abandoned.

Once again Mays, sporting a crash helmet and visor instead of his familiar black beret, had used the two ERAs to be first and second fastest. More 1500cc ERAs took third BTD (Dennis Scribbans) and fourth BTD (Peter Whitehead), with Goodacre's Austin fifth. There was another modern Grand Prix car present in the shape of Hans Ruesch's ex-Scuderia Ferrari Alfa Romeo, together with T.P. Cholmondeley-Tapper's monoposto Maserati 3-litre, but in the wet conditions they did not shine. Yet another intriguing Shelsley Special made its first

appearance: Robert Waddy's Fuzzi had one motorcycle engine driving the front wheels and another driving the rears. It both won its class and set fastest unsupercharged time of day.

It was a huge relief when, for the June 1937 meeting, the weather served up hot sun and clear skies. But even if it had rained the paddock would have been a better place to be. Over the winter it had been given a proper hard surface, and there were now smart rows of roofed wooden bays to provide shelter for each competing car. Nearly 70 years later, they are there still. Also, to speed up the meeting, a return road had been built, although "road" is rather a flattering term for the rough track that had been cleared through the

woods to the left of the hill. There was new electric timing equipment, using a spoon-shaped "hockey stick" which was placed under one front wheel and then, when the car began its run, was snatched away before the rear wheels ran over it. Thus, as the device was triggered by the front wheel, a driver could start in his or her own time, rather than having to move as soon as the lights changed. The innovations were not without their teething problems, however. The timing equipment proved troublesome at first, and a private car trying to descend via the new return road turned over and blocked it for several hours.

Friday was still given over to practice, but the Saturday morning runs were now for "unseeded"

drivers who had to qualify for the afternoon runs, to thin out the slower folk before the main business of the day. The Mays equipe arrived with R4B now in 1500cc Zoller-blown form, with independent front suspension. They'd come hotfoot from the Isle of Man, where Mays had finished second in the RAC road race in Douglas on the Thursday, and the ERA needed a hasty change of gear ratios in the paddock.

Conditions were perfect for Mays to break his own record, but – with the new timing gear recording hundredths of a second instead of merely to the nearest one-fifth of a second – he was 0.09sec outside it on his first run. But his second run did the job in 39.09sec. Bert Hadley's twin-cam Austin

Land Speed Record hero Sir Malcolm Campbell put on a brave show in the big old V12 Sunbeam at the May 1935 meeting.

Dense crowds at the Esses in May 1935 watch the SSK Mercedes of David Scott-Moncrieff.

Seven set second BTD, climbing both times in a brilliant 40.83, 0.06sec quicker than Fane's Frazer Nash. John Bolster was fourth overall and fastest unblown car in a 42.24sec climb which was, said *The Motor*, "a miracle of wheel-winding". Writing in *The Autocar*, Sammy Davis pointed out that during the course of *Bloody Mary*'s hectic climb she had travelled "a considerable distance more than the official thousand yards". It was a good day for the Bolsters, for the former Barbara Skinner was fastest lady with her supercharged Morris. From Italy came a future Grand Prix great, Luigi Villoresi, with a supercharged 1500 Maserati 6CM. Smart in immaculate suit and tie, he climbed in 44.29sec.

Mays was a rare absentee from the September 1937 meeting, busy winning the Phoenix Park

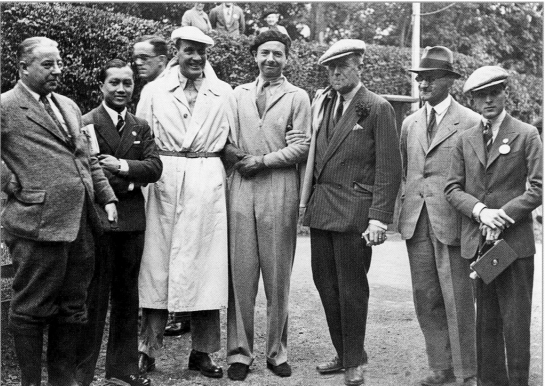

ABOVE: May Millington takes Jucker's single-seater Alta into the Top Ess in September 1936. Seconds later she crashed heavily at the top of the hill.

LEFT: Lining up for the camera at the June 1936 Shelsley are (from left) steward C.R.M. Parr, Prince Bira, Hans Stuck, Raymond Mays, steward Earl Howe, and Leslie Wilson and his son Roger.

A.F.P. Fane breaks the record in September 1937 with a superb run in the single-seater Frazer Nash.

Grand Prix in Ireland on the same day, and the weather once again encouraged records. A young Bristol driver called Joe Fry was making his first appearance, and thus had to qualify during the morning. His car was an 1100cc rear-engined Shelsley Special, built by his cousin David Fry and Dick Caesar and called the Freikaiserwagen.

But BTD was taken by the stylish A.F.P. Fane in his twin-supercharged single-seater Frazer Nash. The timing gear malfunctioned on his first run, so he got another go, and produced a startling 38.77 seconds – a new record, and a new name on the BTD trophy after six inscriptions for Mays. "When the speakers came through with his time," reported *The Autocar*, "there was a complete hush, and then a belated clap and cheer, so surprised was the crowd". Charlie Martin's red-painted 1500cc ERA, the ex-works R3A, was second quickest, Martin becoming only the third man ever to break 40sec. His 39.67 was "a most

hair-raising matter to watch", said *The Motor*. Kenneth Evans was an impressive third in his 2.9-litre monoposto Alfa. The works Austin 7s continued to be astonishingly quick, with Charles Goodacre and Bert Hadley testing the new timing gear by being four-hundredths apart on 40.70 and 40.74. These beautifully built single-seaters were like miniature Grand Prix cars, and their Murray Jamieson-developed engines, tiny jewel-like supercharged twin-cams of just 750cc, were said to produce 100bhp. Kay Petre's blue-painted supercharged sidevalve Austin single-seater shaved her own ladies' record by 0.02sec. After *Bloody Mary* suffered mechanical ills, Joe Fry's little monster was best unsupercharged car on 42.58sec. Surprisingly, three factory V12 Delahayes were entered. Unsurprisingly, they didn't turn up.

For 1938 Mays was intent on regaining his record, and arrived for the May meeting with ERA R4 now to D specification and in bored-out 1750cc

ABOVE: The little twin-cam Austin 7s were real racing cars, and very quick. This is Bert Hadley climbing in 40.74sec in September 1937.

LEFT: Two motorcycles wheel to wheel during the private experiment three weeks after the June 1939 Shelsley.

ABOVE: Aviatrix Amy Johnson in the Esses in her BMW 328, May 1938.

RIGHT: Amy's long-distance solo flights had made her a national celebrity. Here she meets an admirer in the paddock.

form. But in the first runs the amazing Bert Hadley Austin managed 40.09sec, while Mays and Fane dead-heated for second, 0.04sec slower. Come the second runs Fane blew a head gasket and crossed the finish line in a cloud of steam, Hadley brushed the bank and was slower, and Mays dug deep. But the ERA nearly got away from him on the notorious concrete patch of surface on the kink before the Esses: while his 38.9sec was BTD, Fane kept the record. John Bolster turned up with his latest special, an extraordinary device with four 1-litre JAP engines, but only managed one halting run. An innovation was a class for pre-1914 racing cars, which demonstrated how the Shelsley surface had improved since the early days: the 47.96 by Anthony Heal's 10-litre Grand Prix FIAT

Hans Ruesch's 8C Alfa was hefty for Shelsley, but more than a decade later Dennis Poore would be hillclimb champion with the same car.

The shadow of the coming war hangs over the June 1939 meeting as Raymond Mays lowers the record again, to 37.37sec.

was more than 5sec under Higginson's 1913 record. Popular among the crowds was aviatrix Amy Johnson, having her first motoring competition with a BMW 328.

In September it all went Mays' way. R4D was now in full 2-litre guise and, after Fane's Frazer Nash snapped its supercharger drive, the ERA had the meeting to itself, achieving a new sub-38 record with a superb climb in 37.86sec. Hadley was second on 40.05sec, an Austin 7 best and 0.31 sec faster than the single-seater Frazer Nash of promising youngster Barry Goodwin. A notable fourth overall was the latest Skinner Special, its Morris Minor chassis now powered by a 4-litre straight-eight Hudson unit. Peter Skinner's 41.22sec was a record for unsupercharged Shelsley Specials that would stand until the post-war days.

Two meetings were scheduled as usual for 1939, but of course the September event never took place. This left unrealised an exciting plan to run motorcycles in pairs, actually racing each other up the hill, after a successful dummy run with four motorcyclists watched by club officials. By the June meeting the national mood was gloomy, war clouds were gathering and, despite perfect weather, the crowd was smaller than usual. Raymond Mays was there of course, with R4D now painted black, for he had parted company with the ERA concern and its backer Humphrey Cook. Two un-named friends had come up with the funds to allow Ray to buy R4D, complete with both engines and spares. And it was only right, in this final pre-war Shelsley, that he should notch up his sixth outright record in the memorable time of 37.37sec. Three-seven-three-seven would remain Shelsley's magic mark for a decade.

Fane's "Frash" was healthy enough to set second BTD almost 1.5sec slower, with Bob Ansell's ERA and the inevitable Bert Hadley next up. Other worthy climbs came from Arthur Baron, whose glorious Type 59 Bugatti beat Hans Ruesch's big Grand Prix Alfa 8C by half a second; Wilkie Wilkinson, whose Riley was fastest unsupercharged car; and Sammy Newsome, whose stripped SS100 climbed in 42.85s. But the final record of the day, and of the era, was set by Dorothy Stanley-Turner, in Bob Cowell's ex-Johnny Wakefield Alta: she brought the ladies' record down a bit further, to 43.4sec.

And then Shelsley Walsh fell silent for seven long years.

BIRTH OF THE CHAMPIONSHIP 1946–1959

Through the dark days of war, the Midland Automobile Club maintained its standing among the pillars of the locally-based motor industry. The membership list now included names like Bill Lyons of Jaguar, Victor Riley, the brothers Jensen, Miles Thomas who ran Morris for Lord Nuffield, and John Black of Standard. In June 1945, just a few weeks after VE Day heralded the end of fighting in Europe, Leslie Wilson and a small group of Midland AC officials, plus Raymond Mays, travelled to the Teme Valley to make a tour of inspection of the hill. They found that the road surface had deteriorated badly, and the banks and undergrowth had run wild. But the organisers' huts and paddock shelters were all intact, and it was clear that, with a lot of concentrated effort, Shelsley Walsh could come back to life.

Work started at once, and the first Shelsley of the new era was scheduled for early June 1946. Conrad Milner, the hill's maintenance man, had been employed since 1929 – and was still there 48 years later! Along with a handful of labourers, he shouldered most of the work. They were joined by a couple of German prisoners of war who had

OPPOSITE: Ken Wharton clips the Top Ess drain with the supercharged Cooper-JAP on his record-breaking September 1951 run. It was the first climb to break 37 seconds.

LEFT: Raymond Mays and ERA R4D were the dominant force in immediate post-war hillclimbing. This was his June 1948 BTD.

Talented George Abecassis was a rare visitor to Shelsley, but his supercharged Alta nearly beat Mays in the first post-war meeting.

been billeted on the farm and opted to stay on in the area. Despite shortages, rationing, and the endless difficulties and red tape of a country slowly recovering from a long war, no fewer than 117 cars entered the June meeting. There was qualifying during the morning runs to weed out the slower cars for the afternoon.

An enormous crowd of hillclimb-starved enthusiasts – according to one estimate, as many as 14,000 – managed to get themselves to Shelsley to watch. The police reported five-mile queues on the approaches to the hill, and at 4pm there was still a line of more than 1000 people waiting to pay to get in. Sadly, the weather was perhaps the worst ever, with torrential rain and ankle-deep mud everywhere. Drains overflowed, and rivers of water rushed down the hill. The old return road was unusable, the telephone system broke down, and the meeting began to run very late. But still, until the final runner splashed up the hill at almost 8pm, the spectators huddled up the hillside in the rain, hungry for glimpses of the kinds of cars and drivers that had been unseen for so long.

Even if, sadly, some of the names hadn't survived the war – Spitfire pilot A.F.P. Fane among them – many of the familiar faces were there. Inevitably Raymond Mays and R4D set BTD, while Basil Davenport was back at Shelsley after 15 years

away to clock best unsupercharged time in a fresh incarnation of *Spider*. George Abecassis kept Mays honest by beating his first climb with the 1500cc Alta single-seater, and ended up with second BTD.

At the second post-war meeting, run in early October, there was a major innovation: the acceptance of a batch of motorcycles on the entry list. Despite the July 1939 experiment they were running singly, but now Raymond Mays had opposition from a new quarter. The fastest of them, the 500cc Triumph twin of Manx GP winner Ernie Lyons, climbed in 39.44sec on its first run, beating Mays' best effort by 0.13sec. But it was raining as Lyons took his second run, and he lost the Triumph on the approach to the Esses and came off. Abecassis, using a Type 59 Grand Prix Bugatti instead of his Alta, was again second to Mays among the car drivers, and third was a 1500cc ERA in the hands of the bespectacled Leicestershire garage owner, Bob Gerard.

In 1947 the sport of hillclimbing came of age when the RAC, as the country's governing body of motorsport, inaugurated the British Hillclimb Championship. For this first season there were five rounds, with a complex scoring system which penalised each driver for every fifth of a second that he was slower than BTD. The June meeting was Shelsley's round. Yet again it was wet, yet again the crowd was enormous, and yet again Mays dominated, with a 41.5. Ken Hutchinson clocked an impressive second BTD, albeit 1.7sec slower, in his recently acquired ex-Scuderia Ferrari Alfa Romeo P3. Prince Bira finally made his Shelsley debut with an 8CM Maserati, decked out in the blue and yellow racing colours of Siam. He finished third, ahead of Gerard's ERA and John Bolster, back with the immortal twin-engined *Bloody Mary*. Sydney Allard's new single-seater made its first Shelsley appearance, using an air-cooled 3.7-litre Steyr V8 engine originally developed in Austria for military use, but it was only tenth quickest. The 500cc Formula 3 movement was gathering momentum, and the first two Coopers to be built appeared at this meeting in the hands of John Cooper and Eric Brandon; but Colin Strang's home-brewed 500 won the class. That season, Mays went on to be the first British Hillclimb Champion by a comfortable margin.

The weather finally relented for the September meeting, but Mays failed by 0.32sec to beat his own record. It was generally agreed that the hill was bumpier than it had been before the war, particularly on the approach to the Esses. Gerard's ERA was second this time with an excellent 38.55, half a second quicker than Dennis Poore, who had bought the ex-Hans Ruesch Alfa Romeo 8C-35 and painted it green. In fact, the paddock was full of great pre-war Grand Prix cars – Roy Salvadori, Tony Rolt and Ken Hutchison all had their Alfas, Bira and Ken McAlpine their Maseratis – but the real shape of things to come emerged among the 500s, for the little Coopers of Brandon and Cooper turned the tables on Strang.

It was Mays again in the June 1948 meeting, but he was still half a second slower than his pre-war record. One of his closest challengers was expected to be ERA R6B in the hands of Bob Gerard, but Mr Bob had had a big accident the week before at the Stanmer Park event near Brighton. Arriving at the finish line having just broken the hill record, he found the stopping

Bob Gerard elbows his ERA into the Esses to take third BTD in June 1948.

Sensation of the
September 1949 meeting
was George Brown's
outright record astride
his Vincent Black
Lightning. No other
motorcycle before or since
ever held the record.

distance totally inadequate, and bounced off several other competitors' cars in the top paddock before coming to rest. So he came to Shelsley in one of his other ERAs, which handled less well, and was pushed down to third place by Dennis Poore, who was now really getting the hang of the big old Alfa.

Meanwhile John Cooper had fitted a 1000cc JAP twin in the back of a slightly lengthened Cooper chassis, and was fifth fastest overall and best unsupercharged car. John Bolster's elderly *Bloody Mary*, one of the parked cars damaged in the Gerard accident, had needed a rapid front-end rebuild. As a result the old queen was handling much better, and the brave Bolster turned in a best-ever 40.97sec climb. *Spider* was suffering from an intermittently slipping clutch, so Basil Davenport resorted to a typically make-do mod. He tied one end of a rope to the clutch lever and the other end to his wrist, and when the clutch started to slip he yanked his arm back to make it

grip. This meeting was the opening round of the second British Hillclimb Championship, which had now reverted to a more conventional system of points-scoring – and by the end of the season Mays had won the title again, but this time by just one point from Poore.

Conditions for the September meeting were perfect, and the startline area had been resurfaced. Nine drivers broke 40sec – but still Mays was 0.15sec off his pre-war record. As well as hillclimbing *Bloody Mary*, John Bolster was by now racing Peter Bell's ERA, R11B. He drove both at this meeting, and broke his own class record in *BM*, but snapped both the ERA's half-shafts as he left the line on his first run. Gerard's and Mays' mechanics helped Bolster's man George Boyle to change them, and R11B was just about ready for his second run. Thoroughly wound up by now, the moustachioed farmer (journalism and broadcasting were still to come) tore up the hill, glanced off the bank out of the Top Ess, and

crossed the line in 38.16sec – a brilliant second BTD ahead of Poore and Peter Walker's 1500cc ERA. The Freikaiserwagen reappeared in radically rebuilt form, with a lighter chassis and more power from the supercharged 1100cc Blackburne twin, and Joe Fry set a new Shelsley Specials record in 38.43sec.

An important Shelsley newcomer, with a Cooper 500, was a tousle-haired dentist's son named S.C. Moss, who had just had his 19th birthday. He'd tried to enter the May Shelsley, but Leslie Wilson deemed his experience insufficient and turned him down. In the interim he'd had a lot of success in hillclimbs and the few available circuit races, and there was now no question of not accepting his entry. The Moss equipe was impressive: an elderly but immaculate cream Rolls-Royce towed a cream horsebox, which disgorged a gleaming cream Cooper-JAP. Young Stirling, in neatly laundered white overalls, was helped by his parents Alfred and Aileen, both of whom had

motorsport credentials, and Don Müller, a German ex-prisoner of war who worked on the Moss farm. None of this would have added up to much had the boy not shown talent, but he beat all the 500cc establishment and set a new class record. *The Autocar* spoke of his "sheer genius in cornering". He would not be the first, or the last, to start in hillclimbing and make it all the way to Formula 1 greatness. Another future F1 driver entered at Shelsley that day was the young Harry Schell, with a pretty little 1100 Cisitalia single-seater: in the event Schell was unable to appear, and the car was driven by Russian émigré Zora Arkus-Duntov. He would later move to the USA and run the Chevrolet Corvette programme for General Motors.

On 11 June 1949 the long-standing three-seven three-seven barrier was broken at last. But the real sensation was that the new record-holder wasn't Raymond Mays. Mays did beat his own record by the smallest possible margin – 0.01sec – and this

Sydney Allard's Steyr-powered single-seater took him to the 1949 British Hillclimb Championship.

was after R4D's Zoller blower gave trouble in practice. His mechanic Ken Richardson put the ERA in its truck, drove to Lincolnshire, worked on it all night and had it back in Worcestershire ready for Mays' first run. The ferocious Freikaiserwagen now had two-stage supercharging and about 140bhp to propel less than 7cwt, and Fry climbed in a scintillating 37.35sec. Mays, having lost his long-standing record, did his utmost to respond, and achieved 37.36sec – beaten by a hundredth of a second. For the first time in more than 20 years, a Shelsley Special had taken the Shelsley record. *Motor Sport* observed:

Fry's second climb was a model of how to do it, leaving only a very slender safety margin. The Freikaiserwagen's acceleration up the straight, *tyres nearly alight and the two-stage V-twin sounding absolutely right, had to be seen to be believed, and could only just be believed even then, bringing exclamations of joy from the lips of even blasé pressmen.*

Thus Joe Fry joined the elite, and Mays' days as a Shelsley record-holder were over. Meanwhile young Moss now had an 1100cc Cooper, and his best climb, 38.57sec, was the fastest ever by an unsupercharged car. At the September meeting he reduced that further to 38.19sec: "once seen, never forgotten", said one reporter. This time Fry was again fastest, but five-hundredths off his own record. Dennis Poore hustled the big Alfa up in an exceptional 37.47sec, but Mays could do no better than third on 37.56sec.

Dennis Poore, who never bothered with a crash helmet until RAC regulations demanded it, extracted great things from the ex-Ruesch Alfa 8C, culminating in the 1950 British title.

After his September 1950 BTD, Poore is congratulated by Leslie Wilson and MAC chairman C.R.M. Parr.

However, all of them were soundly beaten by the motorcyclist George Brown, whose 1000cc Vincent-HRD Black Lightning climbed in 37.13sec. For the first, and only, time the outright Shelsley hill record had been taken by a motorbike. Brown had never been to Shelsley before. After his run, when asked over the PA for his impressions of the hill, he replied: "Well, I reckon it's damn dangerous."

As for the Hillclimb Championship that year, it was going Joe Fry's way until he had various mechanical ills at the final round at Prescott. Sydney Allard, whose Steyr-Allard was never a real front-runner at Shelsley, had been very quick almost everywhere else, and he ended up taking the title from Poore – with Stirling Moss a surprise third.

As motorsport prepared for the new decade, several of the top contenders were planning ever more potent machinery. The Freikaiserwagen team proposed turning their V-twin Blackburne engine into a W-triple, with even bigger superchargers and a self-change gearbox. Raymond Mays, despite his preoccupations with the BRM project, was having a lighter and more modern car built around the faithful ERA engine. Sydney Allard was working on a lightweight four-wheel-drive sprint car, still using air-cooled Steyr

power. But, as it turned out, none of these exciting projects ever saw the light of day. Mays did enter his new car for the June 1950 Shelsley but, BRM-like, it was unfinished, so he had to fall back on his faithful ERA R4D – and with it he took one last Shelsley BTD, his 21st.

It was a hot day, and melting tar put a new hill record out of reach, but Mays' 38.61 was 0.25sec quicker than Poore in the Alfa. Third quickest was Ken Wharton, the Smethwick driver who'd previously campaigned his own Special, based around an Austin 7 chassis and a supercharged MG J4 engine. Already in his 30s, he now had a 1000cc Cooper, and was really making his mark – as well as showing his versatility in trials, where he won three consecutive British Championships, and in international rallying. The Freikaiserwagen had a big accident at Crossing, running up the bank and looping the loop. Joe Fry was tossed into the road, but scrambled up with nothing worse than a cut hand. In the first-aid tent the nurse offered Joe a sal volatile, but he replied that he'd prefer a brandy and soda. Sadly, it was to be his last Shelsley. The Freikaiserwagen was mended in time for the Blandford hillclimb the following month, but once again the enormously potent little car turned over, and this time Fry was fatally injured.

Dennis Poore was already crowned the 1950 British Hillclimb Champion by the time he came to the September Shelsley, so it was fitting that he set his one and only Shelsley BTD that day. Only the first runs were dry, and his 37.74 was 0.3sec faster than an on-form Sydney Allard, who seemed to have got to grips with Shelsley at last in the Steyr-powered single-seater. His time was a new unsupercharged record. John Bolster had retired from racing after a big accident in Peter Bell's ERA during the 1949 British Grand Prix, so Bell offered R11B to Ken Wharton, who demonstrated the shape of things to come by edging out Raymond Mays by 0.13sec. Another new name was Kidderminster garage owner's son Peter Collins, who was building a reputation in F3 on the circuits. His Cooper now had a 1260cc twin, and his 39.76sec was fifth fastest climb of the day. Collins moved on from hillclimbs once his circuit racing career took off; but, like Moss, he had gained useful early experience on the hills.

An innovation at this meeting was a class for genuine, fully road-equipped production sports cars, for which Allard, Frazer Nash and Aston Martin each sent three works entries. J.V.S. Brown was persuaded by his girlfriend, Miss H.M. Holden, to let her have a go in his HRG, even though she'd never driven in anger before. She beat him in both the dry and wet runs, and won the class. "Now

On the beat: a uniformed constable watches Ken Gregory's Kieft being worked on as the 500s line up in the paddock, June 1950. Car No. 10 is Don Truman's Bardon-Turner.

we'd like to see her do some circuit racing," pleaded *Motor Sport*, but history doesn't relate whether Brown ever gave her another drive. Overall, the Frazer Nash Le Mans Replicas of Donald Pitt, Tony Crook and Jack Newton beat the Jaguar XK120s, led by Peter Walker, for the production class team prize, but there was some glory for Jaguar when the Alpine Rally-winning XK NUB120, with Ian and Pat Appleyard aboard, made a climb of honour.

The Wharton era really began in 1951. He now had a lighter Cooper with a supercharger hung on its 996cc JAP engine, while continuing with his earlier car in 500cc form. The June meeting celebrated the Midland AC's half-century with a variety of veteran and vintage cars making climbs, including Rupert Instone in the Daimler with which his father had set Shelsley's first BTD. But at the business end Wharton took a crucial 0.08sec off Fry's car record with a brilliant 37.27sec. Poore was second in the big Alfa with a personal best of 37.38sec, while third was the AJB, Archie Butterworth's Shelsley Special, a confection that combined a Steyr engine and a Jeep 4wd chassis. The talented Wharton won two other classes with the 500 Cooper and the Bell ERA.

By the September meeting Wharton was already crowned 1951 British Hillclimb Champion, the first of four consecutive titles. At Shelsley he

Works Jaguar at Shelsley: Peter Walker set a new sports car record with this C-type at the singleton 1952 meeting.

carved a big chunk off his own car record with the supercharged Cooper and disposed of George Brown's outright record at last, dipping into the 36s for the first time with a 36.62sec climb. "It was", said one report, "driving that amounted to artistry." Then he got into ERA R11B and set second BTD with that. His extraordinary 37.01 with the old car finally consigned all Raymond Mays' efforts with R4D to the history books, and underlined Wharton's reputation as the best hillclimber of his era. Poore in the Alfa actually did 36.92 in practice, but his best on the day was 37.55. Allard in the Steyr-Allard and Collins in the big-engined Cooper were next up, and Wharton exchanged his smaller Cooper for the Stirling Moss Kieft-Norton to win the 500 class. Tony Crook got down to a splendid 41.46 with his maroon Le Mans Replica Frazer Nash, 0.14sec quicker than Sydney Allard's Allard J2 and a new production sports car record. Archie Butterworth's AJB nudged the bank at Crossing, lost its right rear wheel, and somersaulted over the bank to the left, throwing the driver out. He was badly injured, but eventually recovered fully.

Pre-war, only Brooklands and Donington competed seriously with Shelsley for spectators' attention. By the start of the 1950s, however, circuit racing was growing fast: Silverstone and Goodwood were in full swing, and up and down the country other disused wartime airfields were being pressed into use. Hillclimb crowds were lower than they had been, so for 1952 the MAC decided to move the first Shelsley of the year from its traditional June date to April, believing that running the event in the school holidays would

swell the gate. But the change was poorly communicated to the competitors. By the closing date for entries there were too few to make up a proper event and, to the club's embarrassment, it had to be cancelled.

So the August meeting was Shelsley's only 1952 event. In a year in which Ken Wharton won every round of the Hillclimb Championship, it provided further proof of his crushing superiority. The result was a mirror image of the previous one: BTD in the Cooper, second BTD in the ERA, 500cc class winner in the Kieft. His Frazer Nash Le Mans Replica won the 3-litre production sports car class as well, but the outright sports car record fell to Peter Walker in a works Jaguar C-type like the one with which he and Peter Whitehead had scored that historic victory at Le Mans the previous year. Walker's 41.14sec was seventh BTD. Third overall was the 1100 Cooper of rising talent Michael Christie, the tall, elegantly-dressed man whose tuning business, Alexander Engineering, was to become highly successful in the decades to come. Fourth was another future automotive name, Air Vice-Marshal Don "Pathfinder" Bennett, who later built the homely Fairthorpe cars but this time was in a Cooper-Vincent. Although Rupert Instone's 1100cc Special *Djinn* hit both banks at the Esses, his only injury was a bloody nose. *The Autocar* reported that Instone "tapped his own claret by banging his nose violently on his wrist-watch". Among the motorcycles, George Brown's Vincent was fastest again, while veteran *Autosport* photographer Frankie Penn reckoned the sight of Pip Harris' bike and sidecar coming through the Esses "with his passenger perched almost on his

Ken Wharton takes old R4D to yet another outright record in June 1954.

neck" had been excelled only by Stuck's Auto Union climb in the wet 16 years before.

In 1953, for the first time, both Shelsley meetings counted towards the Hillclimb Championship. In contrast to Moss and Collins, Wharton was determined to remain loyal to hillclimbing, despite being in increasing demand for circuit racing. He arrived at the June meeting in a somewhat battered state: the previous weekend, racing at Albi in the BRM team with Fangio and Gonzalez , his V16 had thrown a tread, hit a telegraph pole and cart-wheeled. Shelsley was on the Saturday of the Dutch Grand Prix weekend, so Wharton, nursing his bruises, practised his Cooper-Bristol at Zandvoort on Friday, missed Saturday practice so he could fly to England to do Shelsley, and then returned to Holland on Saturday night for the GP the next day.

It was worth the trip. Wearing, as ever, his distinctive yellow shirt, he shaved 0.02sec off his hill record in the supercharged Cooper, and yet again finished second to himself in the ERA. Michael Christie, in a Kieft this time, was third. The indefatigable Wharton also managed to win the three-car team award all by himself, in Cooper, ERA and 500cc Arengo. Leslie Wilson decided this wasn't playing the game, but Ken pointed out that there was nothing in the rules to prevent it. Thereafter the wording was changed to require three different drivers as well! The sports car record went again at this meeting, first to George Abecassis in the brand new HWM-Jaguar sports car, and then by a further 0.19sec to Cyril Wick's lightweight ex-works Allard J2.

The most remarkable time at the August 1953 meeting was set by Wharton again, but in practice.

BRM were persuaded to send the BRM V16 to Shelsley for Wharton to demonstrate, and in the dry on Friday he took this dramatically unsuitable car up the hill in an astonishing 37.97sec. But Saturday's weather was dreadful – one of the magazine reports was headlined *Shelsley Squelch* – and no-one broke 40sec. Wharton was first and second as usual, but in the conditions he was quicker in the ERA than the supercharged Cooper. Battling with Michael Christie for third spot were two more up-and-coming names in V-twin Coopers, Shenstone publican "Dick" Henderson and young farmer Tony Marsh in the ex-Peter Collins car, with the place going to Henderson.

The 1954 season was set up as a Wharton-versus-Christie battle. Wharton had forsaken Peter Bell's ERA and bought the immortal ex-Mays R4D from its previous owner Ron Flockhart, preparing it for the season with infinite care. Bell promptly put R11B at Christie's disposal, and bought a new supercharged Cooper-JAP for him as well. At the June meeting, in perfect weather, Wharton's climb in Mays' old ERA was inch-perfect, and a masterpiece of control. Once more R4D, now almost 20 years old, held the hill record, in a stunning 36.58sec. Raymond Mays himself had come to Shelsley as a spectator and was clearly delighted – and even more so when Wharton insisted that Mays took the old black car up the hill on a demonstration run. The prolific Wharton also demonstrated the Mk II V16 BRM.

Michael Christie was almost as impressive, taking second overall in Bell's ERA. When the duo changed to their Coopers, Christie was quicker than Wharton by 0.16sec. Tony Marsh broke his transmission on the line for his first run but on his second, using a gearbox borrowed from Wharton, he beat both of them to take a brilliant third BTD. Half a century later, Marsh would still be tackling Shelsley with undiminished vigour.

Michael Christie blasts off the line in Peter Bell's supercharged Cooper-JAP, June 1954.

This, incidentally, was the first Shelsley meeting to be held on a Sunday. Traditional concerns were addressed by the vicar of the little church next to the paddock holding a brief service, and a collection was taken among the spectators.

Two months later another definitive page of Shelsley history was written when Wharton turned in a simply magical climb in the old ERA to take the record under 36 seconds for the first time. His 35.80 was the last time a front-engined car would hold the hill record, and it would stand for four years. It remained fastest-ever ERA time until the different context of a smoother surface, more efficient tyre compounds and further engine development would see it beaten some three decades later. Christie was competing with three cars that day – Bell's ERA, Bell's supercharged 1100 Cooper, and a works-loaned unsupercharged 1100 Cooper. He got second BTD with the latter, and third BTD with the ERA. Tony Crook in his ultra-light, supercharged, cycle-winged maroon Cooper-Bristol set a new sports car record in

39.06sec, and Don Parker's 39.79sec with his crimson Kieft was a new 500cc record.

After four consecutive British Championship titles, Ken Wharton missed several of the early 1955 rounds, having been burned in a fiery crash in his Vanwall at Silverstone. The June Shelsley was wet, and even in Wharton's absence Christie was denied BTD, for Tony Marsh coped superbly with the slippery conditions in his unblown Cooper. Christie was second in Bell's ERA, with Dick Henderson third.

Wharton was back, driving both ERA and Cooper, for the August meeting, which celebrated Shelsley's half-century. But perhaps his punishing schedule across so broad a spectrum of motorsport was beginning to put him at a disadvantage against the hillclimb specialists, as he was beaten for the first time in a straight fight. The margin was tiny: in R4D he was 0.07sec slower than Tony Marsh, who was 0.28 off the record with his Mk 8 Cooper-JAP. With the Cooper, Wharton took third BTD, while Christie was beaten for

Big, hairy sports cars have always been a feature of Shelsley. This is Cyril Wick's Cadillac-powered Allard J2 at the Esses in 1954.

fourth place by Jerseyman Bill Knight in yet another Cooper. As part of the hill's 50th anniversary celebrations Fred Bennett climbed the hill in his 6.5 horsepower 1903 Cadillac, the same car with which he'd competed in August 1905. While he and others epitomised the past, the Rover gas turbine car, JET 1, epitomised the possible future.

As for the championship, the season ended with Marsh and Wharton tying on points. The rules said any tie should be resolved by the RAC deciding who had put up the most meritorious performance. Despite Wharton having missed several rounds, this invidious decision was resolved in favour of Marsh who, at 24, became the youngest British Hillclimb Champion yet.

The move to Sunday meetings had helped the gate but incurred the wrath of members of the Lord's Day Observance Society. Under pressure from them the 1956 events were moved back to Saturday. That, plus dreadful weather, contributed to a poor gate for the June meeting, but the

renewed battle between Wharton, Christie and Marsh was a good one, and Wharton showed tremendous class in the wet to get R4D up the slippery hill almost a second clear of everyone else. Christie's Cooper was second, Wharton's Cooper third and Marsh's Cooper fourth. A fortnight later the MAC held a members' invitation meeting, for sports and road cars only. Tony Marsh took this easily with his recently-acquired manx-tail Cooper-Climax sports-racer from Bill Knight's similar car. His 38.80sec climb was actually a new sports car hill record by a large margin, but as this was not a full Shelsley meeting it was never recognised.

The August meeting started dry but turned wet after the small single-seaters had taken their first runs, and that effectively decided the final order. So Tony Marsh's unblown Cooper took BTD from the Coopers of Wharton and Christie. Marsh's 36.02sec was an 1100cc class record, and his 39.34sec with the Cooper Manx was accepted as a new sports car mark. Another small sports car

Tony Marsh's Shelsley career spans more than half a century and some 15 BTDs, including this one in August 1955 when he first vanquished Ken Wharton.

was a yellow 1172 Ford-powered Lotus 11, borrowed from Colin Chapman by one of his factory workers, N.G. Hill – the same Graham Hill who went on to be a double World Champion in Formula 1. It was raining steadily by the time the bigger racing cars came out and, after his first run in R4D, Wharton declared that Shelsley was more slippery than he had ever known it, although he won his class, of course. He also squeezed in a couple of runs in a Cooper-Jaguar before flying off to Switzerland to drive a Ferrari in the Ollons-Villars mountain hillclimb next day. Sadly it was his last Shelsley: the following January this brave, forceful and always busy driver was killed driving a Ferrari in a race in New Zealand. Meanwhile the consistent, polished Tony Marsh had won his second Hillclimb Championship title.

After three Shelsleys in 1956, there was only one in 1957, run at the end of August – the July meeting had been cancelled because of petrol rationing, introduced in the wake of the Suez Crisis. In an effort to ensure that all entrants in the RAC Hillclimb Championship could compete for their points in comparable conditions, they would henceforth get two extra runs between the first and second class runs – a procedure which would develop into today's Top Twelve run-offs. At the 1957 meeting, on his way to a third consecutive title, Tony Marsh got maximum points, but he couldn't beat the effort at the end of the class runs by Dick Henderson. The ruddy-faced publican was bang on form, and his supercharged Cooper, sporting twin rear wheels in a nostalgic nod to an earlier era, got within .04sec of Wharton's ERA record and beat Marsh's best by 0.43sec. Tommy Sopwith's 39.09sec in the American Lupton Rainwater III's bobtail Cooper was officially a new sports-car record, while Phil Scragg was a fifth of a second slower with his cycle-winged HWM-Jaguar but still set a big-capacity sports car record.

Rain again spoiled the June 1958 meeting, after Marsh had got 0.3sec under Wharton's record in practice. But Tony was quickest anyway, with a newer name taking second place. The eldest of the Boshier-Jones brothers, David, was a Monmouth garage owner who had been a successful 500cc circuit racer, and had also broken the 500cc record at Shelsley in 1954. Now he was concentrating on hillclimbs, with the inevitable 1100cc JAP powering his immaculately prepared pale green Cooper. And it was good to see a Shelsley Special setting third BTD: this was the Farley Special, built by Dr John Farley around a simple ladder chassis with its 1000cc JAP assisted by two chain-driven superchargers. It was driven by the burly, ebullient Chris Summers. Meanwhile the Fairley Special, effectively a Cooper 500 with a supercharged Climax engine fitted transversely across the back of the car, set sixth BTD, driven by the ever-cheerful boss of Fairley Steels in Sheffield, Reg Phillips. The water-cooled engine had no radiator, Reg relying on getting to the top of the hill before it boiled.

A fortnight later there was another members' invitation meeting, which allowed Morgan Plus Four driver Les Yarranton to write his name in the list of Shelsley BTD men, but the serious chaps returned in late August. This was Leslie Wilson's last Shelsley before retiring as MAC secretary after 37 years, and appropriately it was a vintage day. The weather was fine, and at last Ken Wharton's four-year-old record was beaten. Tony Marsh was spending more time circuit racing his Formula 2 Cooper around Europe, but he returned to Worcestershire with his faithful 1100 JAP to claim his first Shelsley record in a smooth, undramatic 35.60sec. Boshier-Jones, who'd been racking up the points in the other championship rounds in Marsh's absence – he would earn his first title that year – took second place 0.73sec slower, and once again the Farley Special was third, Summers climbing in a very brave 36.63sec which was a new Shelsley Specials record. Reg Phillips and the Fairley were fourth this time.

Among several new class records, the most popular was set by Patsy Burt. She achieved 39.03sec with her gleaming pale blue F2 Cooper, which made her the first woman driver to climb Shelsley in under 40sec. In the championship run-offs she reduced this to 38.66, which gave her eighth place points. Tony Marsh brought his F2 Cooper as well, but made a most untypical mistake and lost it approaching the Esses, spinning backwards into the bank. Another driver to get into trouble was Phil Scragg. The Macclesfield industrialist was trying to beat his own class record with the HWM when he mounted the bank approaching the Esses, and seemed sure to turn over before the car thumped down on its wheels again.

Phil Scragg specialised in hairy sports-racing cars. He headed up a company making textile

machinery, and gossip said that his company's board of directors had passed a resolution banning their chairman from either motor racing or driving racing cars. But Phil interpreted "motor racing" as competing on circuits, which allowed him to continue with hillclimbs and sprints, and "racing cars" as single-seaters that could not be driven on the road. So he campaigned an increasingly hairy selection of road-registered sports-racing cars, favouring cycle-winged bodywork which made them easier to place on narrow twisty hills. And he actually drove them to and from meetings, and appeared not to possess a tow car or trailer. Soon after dawn on a Shelsley weekend, wet or dry, this prosperous businessman would thunder into the paddock, bareheaded but with goggles over his glasses, having driven down from Macclesfield.

Phil Scragg's forceful driving of road-registered sports-racing cars enlivened Shelsley Walsh for more than 30 years. This unorthodox approach to the Esses in his HWM-Jaguar was at the August 1958 meeting.

Scragg had started with an early Jaguar XK120 and soon moved on to an ex-Grand Prix Alta, which HWM turned into a Jaguar-powered narrow two-seater for him. In 1956 he replaced the Alta with the last competition car built by HWM, also cycle-winged and Jaguar-powered, and subsequently he bought the open-wheel Lister-Jaguar that had been built for the "Monzanapolis" race and had it converted into sports-racing form. Much later there was an incredible projectile, a Lola T70 with the bodywork removed, its naked monocoque skimpily clothed in a few basic fibreglass panels and with cycle wings over its huge wheels. This monster may not have arrived at each meeting under its own power, but it too was road-registered. With tragic irony, many years later Phil Scragg did die on a race track. Competing in a sprint at Silverstone in his V12 E-type road car, he spun backwards into an earth bank and was killed instantly.

Leslie Wilson's replacement as secretary of the MAC was Gerry Flewitt. It was no secret that, financially, the club had been struggling with Shelsley in recent years. There was now a lot of motorsport up and down the country competing for enthusiasts' attention, and the wet meetings had suffered from dismal gates. After the Lord's Day protests all dates had reverted to Saturdays, and this was at a time when many people worked five-and-a-half day weeks. However for 1959 the MAC, under its president Sammy Newsome,

tackled the problems head-on. Henceforth the meetings would always be on Sunday, and to hell with the protests.

Meanwhile, substantial club funds would be invested in improving the amenities. Spectators arriving for the first 1959 meeting – on Sunday 14 June – found much that was different. Instead of parking beyond the public road and trudging back to the hill with their picnic baskets, they could now park in the orchard, which had been cleared of trees. In the woods up to the Esses, undergrowth had been thinned and some trees felled. Improved paths and steps made the best viewing points more accessible. The hill itself had been completely resurfaced and some of the worst bumps smoothed out, but the weather was very warm and much of the new tar melted, so no really quick times were seen yet.

Reigning champion David Boshier-Jones was fastest, almost 1.4sec off the record, with David Good emerging from the championship runs with second BTD. Good had been featuring well for a while with a beautifully presented Cooper-JAP, his forceful driving apparently totally uncompromised by the fact that his right arm ended in a stump where the elbow should have been. He nonchalantly controlled the steering wheel with this while changing gear with his only hand: as his previous mount was an ERA, the Cooper must have seemed a pussycat by comparison. Tony Marsh's faithful Cooper-JAP was out of action, so

Tony Marsh brought his circuit-racing F2 Cooper-Climax to each of the 1958 Shelsleys, but was always quicker in the Cooper-JAP, and shunted the F2 car at the August meeting.

he brought his Lotus F2 car, which he had radically modified and re-christened the Motus, but Good beat him by just 0.04sec.

BTD at the members' meeting two weeks later was set by George Keylock's supercharged F2 Cooper-Climax, and by the August meeting the new surface had settled in nicely. David Boshier-Jones broke Marsh's year-old record with a climb in 35.47sec, while Marsh, back in the Cooper-JAP and fresh from an international race win at Zeltweg with the F2 Cooper, could only manage 35.70. Good was third, and Summers pipped Henderson for fourth. Ray Fielding's Cooper bobtail shaved 0.02sec off Sopwith's sports car record, while still not beating the time Marsh had set at the 1956 members' event, and Patsy Burt lowered the ladies' record by a further 1.03sec. As expected, Boshier-Jones ended the season champion again, having won every event he entered.

So Shelsley faced the Swinging Sixties in reinvigorated shape – with a new surface, improved spectator facilities and recovering attendances. By now Britain was leading the world in Grand Prix racing, and just as John Cooper's products were humbling the might of Maranello in F1, in hillclimbing the nimble rear-engined cars from Surbiton held sway over the bulkier front-engined machinery. Hillclimb specialists were beginning to take over the top slots from versatile all-round racers like Wharton had been, and Marsh still was, and more and more the technique of driving a car up a narrow bumpy road for a few seconds was being seen as a motorsport discipline that imposed its own special challenges. Thirty years before, the Shelsley hill record had just dipped below 46 seconds. Now it was less than 36 seconds. But it would take another 30 years for it to drop below 26 seconds.

David Boshier-Jones' driving of his Cooper-JAP was as immaculate as his preparation of the car, and brought him three consecutive titles.

THE SHELSLEY SPECIALS

A lot of things make Shelsley Walsh unique, and one of them is the inclusion at most meetings of an award for fastest Shelsley Special. This acknowledges the role played by a bastard breed of machine that goes back almost to the origins of the event. The term "Special", when applied to a car, usually means a machine which has been modified from its original production specification. A humble saloon may be a bit special after the addition of an extra carburettor or the removal of a couple of inches of ground clearance, but a true Special is a home-built car assembled from a motley collection of parts from various sources.

The builder of a Shelsley Special is an ingenious, adventurous type who wants a machine that will do nothing else but go up Shelsley Walsh as fast as possible. Either he is too much of an individualist to go for a conventional car, built by others to a broader set of criteria, or else he can't afford it. In theory, building your own can be cheaper – although it will often end up much, much more expensive. But probably priceless is the immense pride and sense of achievement that comes with competing, and winning, in a car that you have designed, built and gradually developed yourself.

In the search for more speed, greater horsepower, better road-holding and improved braking, or just in a desire to be different, the Special builder often has wild ideas of his own which he is eager to prove to an astonished world. Many of the best Specials down the years have displayed an element of original thinking that

The post-war Freikaiserwagen in full cry, breaking Mays' record in June 1949 with the brave Joe Fry at the wheel.

The archetypal Shelsley Special: Basil Davenport's Spider, on the line in 1926.

borders on eccentricity. The net result of that, apart from the sense of achievement for the driver, is increased entertainment for the spectator. At any given time there will be a type of car, professionally built, which can bring a good driver hillclimbing success at the drop of a chequebook. Down the years it may have been ERA, or Cooper, or McLaren, or Pilbeam. Today it's probably Gould (although David Gould himself started as a hillclimber who built his own car). But a class entirely made up of the same types of car is not so entertaining to watch. At Shelsley, alongside the predictable machines, there have always been devices that looked, sounded and behaved differently. In pre-war days, *The Motor* described it thus:

One of the most attractive things about Shelsley is the perfectly astonishing variety of extraordinary vehicles that make their appearance biennially, and retire into the oblivion of the workshop for the other 363 days of the year. Mostly they have no bodies – no bonnets even – but a bucket seat perched precariously amid a mass of whirling chains. One has a separate single-cylinder motorcycle engine to drive the supercharger. Another has a chain many feet in length threading its way round a great air-cooled V-twin engine: when the unit speeds up, the chain tends to adopt a circular shape. At peak revs it may suddenly fly off with a bang and hurtle through the trees, to the great peril of the bystanders.

The most famous of all Shelsley Specials, and the car that in many ways epitomises the type, was Basil Davenport's *Spider*. This was the first Shelsley Special to set BTD, which it did six times on the trot in the 1920s. An intrinsic part of *Spider*'s character, as with all the best Specials, was the idiosyncratic character that built it, and drove it so bravely. Basil Davenport, a bluff, gruff Northerner, didn't stand on ceremony, and didn't believe in wasting time on spit and polish. Another Special-builder, John Bolster, described *Spider* thus:

> *A high pointed aluminium bonnet, with a clumsy great cylinder sticking out each side, a small pointed aluminium tail, well scratched and dented, a chassis and wheels with very little paint, and a patch or two of rust showing beneath the dirt. Even a car breaker would turn up his nose at this scruffy contraption, this seven times outright victor at the greatest hillclimb in the world.*

Good hillclimb cars need to combine horsepower and light weight, and *Spider* managed this by harnessing a chain-driven GN chassis to a thumping V-twin engine – at first an 1100, then a four-plug, eight-valve 1500 which was constantly developed to find higher revs and more power. The rough body was held on by a few bolts, and lifted off to expose *Spider*'s insides, including the chains that drove its solid back axle.

After terrorising most of his opposition for seven seasons or so, Davenport retired from hillclimbing to concentrate on his business. But he returned after World War II with a born-again *Spider*. It looked much the same, and used many of the same bits, but had a cut-down HRG chassis and a new 2-litre V-twin, and went even faster. Basil's last appearance at Shelsley was in 1974, exactly half a century after his first. On the 100th anniversary of his birth, his widow Lily unveiled a simple memorial to this special Shelsley character, which stands beside the start line. Perpetuating

Raymond Mays' Vauxhall in its final form as the Villiers Supercharge, with huge intercooler alongside the engine.

ABOVE: John Bolster with Bloody Mary making her debut in twin-engined form, September 1934.

RIGHT: Jack Moor battles the yellow and black Wasp up to the Esses, retaining the steering wheel on this occasion.

Gordon Glegg in Dorcas II, which was originally front-wheel-drive and ultimately four-wheel-drive.

Basil's memory even better, both *Spider* models live on. In the brave hands of David Leigh and Martin Spencer, their famous bark has continued to echo up the hill and they have set remarkably quick times.

Raymond Mays' Vauxhall Villiers is an example of a Special which started as a factory car – a 1922 TT Vauxhall – and was gradually developed to such a degree that its origins became almost invisible. It was supercharged by Amherst Villiers, lowered and re-bodied, and ultimately renamed the Villiers Supercharge. In Mays' hands it was the first car to climb Shelsley in under 46 seconds, and it set four BTDs. The car is still active in the hands of former Vintage Sports-Car Club president Julian Ghosh.

John Bolster and his brother Richard were inveterate Specials builders. John's famous *Bloody Mary*, with wooden chassis, was built while he was still a schoolboy and, powered by one and then two JAP engines, continued to be tremendously fast up Shelsley well into the post-war years. It was a tiny car – the steering wheel had to be removed

for the driver to get in – and had one mudguard, judiciously positioned to prevent the driver's right elbow from rubbing on the rear wheel. Initially there was one drum brake, operating on the differential-less rear axle via a hand lever. Later, Austin 7 front stub axles brought the luxury of two more brakes.

Weighing less than 500lbs with one engine, *Mary* was pretty rapid. When, in 1934, Bolster fitted a second JAP engine the result, running on alcohol fuel, was a sensationally fast, frighteningly light 2-litre car, with a power-to-weight ratio of around 300bhp per ton. In 1938 Bolster built a steel-chassis car with no fewer than four V-twin JAP engines giving eight cylinders and four litres. This terrifyingly complex confection never lived up to its promise, however, and after the war the twin-engined *Mary* was dusted off and ran faster than ever, breaking the unsupercharged Shelsley Specials record in 1948.

Richard Bolster had a GN-based Special with a variety of engines, including supercharged MG and

From the minimalist school of Special-building came Jan Breyer's JAP-engined Joystick, later named Salome – the naked lady.

straight-eight American Hudson. He also tried four engines, using single-cylinder Rudge 500cc units, each with a separate chain driving various shafts to meet up with the clutch and final drive. Like his brother he found it hard to make the mixture work – although he did win his class at one Shelsley meeting. Years later, John Bolster wrote:

The Shelsley Specialists, many of them as poor as church mice, simply lived for those two climbs a year, lending spare parts and even working on each others' cars. Their homemade Specials, built on a shoestring, were worked on every night for many months, and once at The Hill they often exploded in a shower of chains and sprockets, but that was life.

On one occasion one of the pioneers of GN Specials, Jack "Moses" Moor, was seen to throw away his steering wheel while taking the Esses at high speed, regaining control by grabbing the remaining stumps of the spokes. Jack's cars were all called Wasp, and painted yellow with black stripes to resemble that insect, but this brought him no luck. One day he was on the starting line, engine revving, when suddenly his clutch spigot bush seized and he made an involuntary getaway. Scattering the marshals, he roared off up the hill but, being a gentleman, he shouted, "Goodbye!"

Typical of the cheerful approach to pre-war Special building were the Glegg brothers, Gordon

ABOVE: Rupert Instone, son of Shelsley's first record holder, with his smart JAP-powered Djinn in 1950.

LEFT: Fuzzi had two engines, one in front of the driver, the other behind. This is Joan Richmond driving the car for owner/builder Robert Waddy.

Alec Issigonis, future Morris Minor and Mini designer, clambers out of the elegant Lightweight Special in the muddy paddock, June 1946.

and Donal. Their various home-brewed cars had rear-wheel-drive, front-wheel-drive and even four-wheel-drive. They were called Dorcas I, Dorcas II and Dorcas III, after the lady in the Old Testament who was "full of good works". Bolster said of the Gleggs:

Whenever their most cherished theories were disproved, to the accompaniment of the thunder of rending metal, they just swept up all the bits they could find and had another go. After their first practice run they were apt to walk up the hill demanding, "Anybody seen a universal joint, a couple of gears and a length of chain?"

Another Special that took little note of convention was Fuzzi, built by a character called Robert Waddy and called after aircrew slang for fuselage. This tiny car had two 500cc JAP engines, one at each end,

each driving the nearest pair of wheels. A rocking throttle pedal allowed the dexterous driver to increase power at the front to kill oversteer or at the rear to cope with understeer – in theory. Rupert Instone, son of the man who set the first Shelsley BTD, produced *Martyr*, with GN chassis and supercharged JAP engine, and later *Djinn*, a neat JAP-powered car. And one Special that no-one could make any jokes about was the Lightweight, an elegantly designed and flawlessly built little single-seater that was the work of Alec Issigonis, later the father of the Mini, and George Dowson. The chassis was a stressed-skin monocoque, far ahead of its time when conceived in the 1930s. The all-independent suspension was by rubber strands in tension and, despite its Austin 7-based engine, the whole machine looked like a miniature Grand Prix car. It was still quick after the war, by which time it was using an experimental 750cc overhead-cam Wolseley engine.

ABOVE: The Freikaiserwagen in original unsupercharged form, about to break the 1100cc class record.

LEFT: Reg Phillips' 1960 Fairley hid its Cooper 500 underpinnings under bluff bodywork. The Climax engine was mounted sideways.

Chris Summers bends the tyres of the twin-supercharged Farley Mk I at the Esses in 1960.

After the war the more successful Specials began to get a little more sophisticated. Sydney Allard didn't count as a Special builder, because he was a motor manufacturer, but his air-cooled single-seater, which won the Hillclimb Championship in 1949, was very much a one-off. It used a drastically modified air-cooled Steyr V8 engine from a German World War II military vehicle, with the air-cooling fan and ducting thrown away because Sid reasoned that, running on alcohol fuel, it wouldn't have time to overheat during the brief blast up a hillclimb. For maximum traction, the driver's seat was right at the back of the narrow body, almost directly over the de Dion-suspended twinned rear wheels. Sid went on to experiment with four-wheel-drive, but never found the same success. Archie Butterworth's AJB, also Steyr-powered, was four-wheel-drive from the start, using transmission parts salvaged from a wartime Jeep.

Very much a private effort, and very much a pure Shelsley Special, was the amazing Freikaiserwagen. In the 1930s David Fry and Dick Caesar, impressed by the rear-engined Auto Union Grand Prix cars, decided to build their own miniature

version. The car's name not only combined the builders' surnames but also perhaps threw an ironic glance at the deteriorating relations between Britain and Hitler's Germany. From the first it used all-independent suspension and an 1100cc Blackburne engine, which was soon supercharged, but in 1938 it was badly damaged in a crash. The bits were resurrected after the war around a new, ultra-light tubular chassis, and later a second supercharger was hooked up. Fiendish attention to weight-saving resulted in a car weighing barely 5cwt and developing almost 140bhp, which gave

a then almost unbelievable power-weight ratio of over 500bhp per ton. David and his cousin Joe both drove it, but as Joe was smaller and lighter he usually got the job, and in 1949 he broke Mays' long-standing Shelsley record with a 37.35. Trying to beat this the following season, he turned over at The Crossing, escaping with a cut hand. The car was mended within days in time for the Blandford event the following weekend, but once again the Freikaiserwagen got out of control, and this time poor Fry was killed. It was the first fatal accident to a car driver in the history of British hillclimbing.

More than 40 years on, the Farley Mk II with Jim Jones at the wheel gets into the 29s at Shelsley.

Specials of various shapes and sizes continued to compete at Shelsley throughout the post-war period, from tiny 500s up to the monstrous *Triangle Flying Saucer*. This immense vehicle combined a four-wheel-drive Daimler Scout Car chassis with a 21-litre Rolls-Royce Kestrel aero engine. The driver, Ted Lloyd-Jones, sat ahead of the naked works between the front wheels. In 1950 he climbed in 46.63sec, the act of a brave man. But the reign of the Cooper meant that it wasn't until 1960 that a Special made BTD again. This was the Fairley of genial Reg Phillips, the boss of Fairley Steels in Sheffield. In a lifetime of hillclimbing, having started with V8 Ford- and Mercury-powered devices (one of which is still campaigned by current owner Alex Brown more than 50 years later), Reg came up with a machine that mixed a chain-driven Cooper 500 chassis with a transverse-mounted, supercharged four-cylinder Climax engine, *sans* radiator. In August 1960, helped by a shower of rain

Karl Schollar's Spectra Mk 7, like the Farley Mk II, uses six small wheels, but differently arranged.

shortly after his run, he beat the field to BTD. Later, at the time that the Jeep-like Mini Moke was a fashion accessory for groovy young things in Swinging London, Reg hillclimbed a hotted-up version which he called the Fairley Poke, before moving on to more conventional machines, from a Chevron sports-racer and a Ferrari to a Sunbeam Lotus saloon and a Peugeot 205.

The Fairley Specials are not to be confused, but often are, with the Farley Specials. These are the brainchildren of Dr John Farley, for whom the burly Chris Summers terrorised the hills in the 1950s with a V-twin JAP-engined device with not one but two chain-driven superchargers. Half a century later, in retirement, Dr John built another, the Farley Mk II, with an 1100cc supercharged V-twin based on a Godden Speedway unit, and an ultra-light chassis using tiny kart wheels with twin rears. Driven by Jim Jones, this device brilliantly beat the half-minute at Shelsley in 2004, hitting an

incredible 100mph into the Esses.

Since the advent of kart racing in the 1960s, several Specials had followed a similar philosophy, notably the Trakstar of Phil Jefferies and Dick Foden. This minute machine was so fast – taking a class record in 31.02sec in 1987 – that some other competitors tried to protest that it wasn't legal. A

decade earlier, another small record breaker was the Voigt-Renwick Special of Peter Voigt, with two-stroke flat-four Konig marine engine.

If you accept the Steyr-Allard as a factory car, the Hillclimb Championship had never been won by a Special – until 1963, when Peter Westbury produced his first Felday, called that after the

The tiny 250cc Trakstar of Phil Jefferies breaks the 500cc racing car class record in June 1987.

mediaeval name of his home village of Holmbury St Mary. This was a Lotus 18/20 chassis, much modified to give the more upright driving position that Westbury felt hillclimbing required, and with a 2.5-litre Daimler V8 engine aspirated by a large supercharger topped by a huge SU carburettor. There were more Feldays, for Westbury went on to become a professional racing car manufacturer – as several other Special builders did after him – but the original Felday-Daimler has been lovingly rebuilt by Ron Welsh and still competes.

In championship terms, the ultimate Special has to be the Marsh. Having won three titles in the 1950s in V-twin Coopers and then returned to hillclimbs with his BRM and Lotus circuit cars, Tony Marsh modified one of the Lotuses and called it a Motus. Then for the 1963 season he built a very small, light Marsh Special with supercharged Climax power. This proved difficult to handle, so for 1965 he lengthened and widened it and fitted an alloy V8 Buick/Oldsmobile engine. This superbly effective machine, in Marsh's perennial mid-green colours with white nose flash, brought him three more consecutive titles, becoming even more competitive when it was completely rebuilt for the 1967 season to incorporate Marsh's own

ingenious part-time four-wheel-drive. Then Tony retired again. The car went through various subsequent owners and was crashed, and rebuilt. Twenty years later Marsh bought it back and went hillclimbing once more. Today, after more than 50 years in the sport, he competes in a very serious 2.5-litre V6 Gould.

Gould is today the top marque in championship hillclimbing, but David Gould started as a Shelsley Special man, creating a beautifully crafted single-seater for his own use. He spent 5000 hours in a one-car garage, designing and building a machine with honeycomb composite monocoque, Kevlar weave bodywork and ground-effects aerodynamics. He even spent three months teaching himself about computers – which were much less universal 20 years ago – so that he could write his own programme to get the suspension geometry right. He and his son Sean both proved to be talented hillclimbers, but David was a race car designer of genius, and when he fitted a 2.5-litre Hart to the Gould and enlisted Chris Cramer as driver, another British Championship title went the way of a Special.

Shelsley Specials continue to be built, thank goodness, and one of the most fascinating of the newer arrivals is the Mannic. Nic Mann is a gifted young engineer who doesn't say a lot, but manages to produce the most extraordinary speed from the most unlikely of vehicles. For many seasons his mount was an innocent-looking Morris Minor which he drove on the road to meetings and used to break records on hills up and down the country. Under the bonnet was a nitrous-injected turbocharged Rover V8 engine producing untold horsepower, and as Nic gradually developed this beast to go faster and faster, he also made it handle surprisingly well.

Once Mann felt that even he couldn't develop the Minor any further, he sold it and bought, for a few hundred pounds, the remains of a crashed Ford Sierra Cosworth saloon. Around the Sierra's engine and four-wheel-drive transmission he built a conventional-looking, fairly bulky clubmen's-type car. Then he added a helicopter starter turbine behind and to the left of the Cosworth four-pot mill. Nic knew that the snag with any turbo is the lag – the time it takes to speed up and deliver the boost required. Even a supercharger, driven off the engine, will only deliver its puff when the revs are there. So he

Peter Westbury's Felday-Daimler took him to his first championship in 1963.

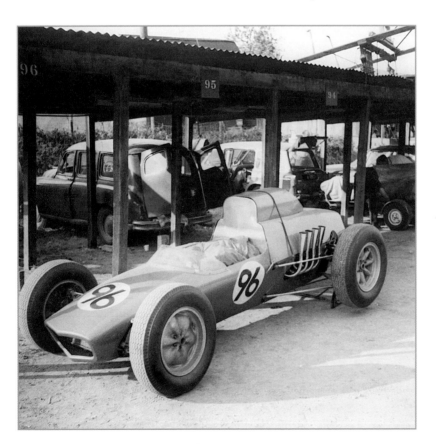

decided to drive the turbo with a separate, high-revving power source, to make instant boost available even from zero engine rpm. With a loud pop and a high-pitched whine, the turbine is fired up as Nic goes to the line for his run, and the car's speed off the line, aided by the four-wheel-drive, is simply awe-inspiring. In August 2004 he set a new supercharged Shelsley Specials record with

the Mannic, and his astonishing time – 26.60sec – was almost in the Championship Top 12 bracket. The Mannic is in every way the descendant of all those other unlikely machines, from *Spider* and *Dorcas* and *Mary* to the Felday and the Marsh. It's the fruit of one man's determination to be different, and in doing so to beat the rest – which is the very essence of the Shelsley Special.

Today's ultimate Shelsley Special is Nic Mann's extraordinary Mannic, with both conventional and turbine engines.

TECHNOLOGY ARRIVES 1960–1979

F or hillclimbing, the 1960s began as the 1950s had ended, with the ubiquitous 1100cc Cooper-JAPs dominant. But during the coming decade the machinery required to set the pace up Shelsley would become very different.

With Tony Marsh now concentrating on circuit racing, David Boshier-Jones was in a class of his own in 1960. At the June meeting the Welshman was the only driver to dip into the 35s, but interestingly the runner-up in the championship runs was Jerseyman Arthur Owen, using a Formula 1 Cooper-Climax in 2.2-litre form – the first time a modern Grand Prix car had challenged for BTD in post-war hillclimbing. It was a foretaste of the sophistication to come. Reg Phillips got the Fairley Special to the top in an excellent 36.38 seconds, a Shelsley Specials record which also earned him third place championship points. The sports cars were in record-breaking mood, too. Phil Scragg was now in the ex-Monza Lister, and set a new mark in 38.43sec, while Josh Randles' Cooper Monaco – later to follow the Scragg route and dispense with full-width bodywork in favour of cycle wings – broke the 2500cc sports car record with 38.73sec.

David Boshier-Jones earned an easy BTD at the members' meeting in late June, but the August meeting was a day of glory for the popular, ever-smiling Reg Phillips. Soon after the Fairley Special had made its first run the rains came: towards the end of the day it dried out again, but even Boshier-Jones was left 0.08sec slower than Phillips' 37.33sec. In the championship runs, with the hill

On 13 June 1971 the elusive half-minute was finally broken at Shelsley, by David Hepworth's own four-wheel-drive car.

August 1961: Tony Marsh storms out of the Esses towards a new record in his BRM, and brings the reign of the Cooper-JAPs to an end.

still damp, the on-form Phillips still managed second to Boshier-Jones, with David Good third from Henderson and Arthur Owen. Having won his third consecutive title, David Boshier-Jones retired from hillclimbing, but the "Bosh" name would continue in the sport in the shape of his younger brother Peter.

Come 1961, the reign of the little Coopers at Shelsley was ended at last. Tony Marsh, still very committed to circuit racing, liked to take in the odd event when he had a free weekend. The Formula 1 capacity limit had now come down to 1500cc, so it was an F1 Lotus 18 that Marsh brought to the June meeting. However his BTD was still 0.39sec off Boshier-Jones' hill record. He said afterwards that the car was over-geared, still

using its Brands Hatch diff ratio from the previous weekend's race. More "big" cars filled the top four places: Geoff Richardson's Cooper-RRA, basically a single-seater Cooper with a Connaught engine, was a surprise second quickest, with Jim Berry's Grand Prix Connaught third and George Keylock's supercharged 1.5 Cooper fourth, although in the championship runs Keylock was second from the 1100 Coopers of Good and Mike Hatton. Among the sports cars, Phil Scragg set another big sports car record in the Lister with 37.72. However this was put into the shade by Peter Boshier-Jones' remarkable 37.50, with only 1098cc powering his little Lola Mk1 – it gave the young Welshman the outright sports car record. Clearly he'd been having home tuition from his brother.

George Keylock's 1.5 Cooper set BTD at the July invitation meeting, an inter-club team handicap affair, and then came the August event, which was officially marking the 60th anniversary of the founding of the Midland Automobile Club. It was one of those magical days, with fine weather, a fascinating entry, and a thrilling new record which broke the 35-second barrier. Tony Marsh brought not only the Lotus 18 but also something even more exciting: his recently-purchased 2.5-litre ex-Formula 1 BRM, a 1960 P48, with three BRM mechanics led by Wilkie Wilkinson in attendance. He was determined to take back his hill record, and all four of his climbs were in the 34s, finally carving the huge margin of 1.06sec off David Boshier-Jones' two-year mark to leave it at 34.41sec. It was the first time a car with an engine of more than 2000cc had held the Shelsley record since Whitney Straight's Maserati 27 years before: never again would a little air-cooled twin be the fastest car up this hill.

But the speed and power of the BRM could not entirely overshadow a tremendous effort by Reg Phillips, the ear-splitting Fairley now wearing new and much tidier bodywork. His 35.08sec was second BTD, faster than Marsh in the Lotus, and it broke his own Shelsley Specials record. In the championship runs a ferocious climb from Chris Summers in the Farley gave him second-place points after George Keylock rolled Tom Norton's supercharged Lotus-Climax at Kennel, and championship leader David Good had his engine seize on the finishing straight. Peter Boshier-Jones was 0.07sec off his record with the little Lola, but still 0.02sec faster than Scragg's Lister.

The motorcycles were running once more, and veteran George Brown, 12 years after he'd set outright BTD at Shelsley, went 0.53sec quicker on his Vincent to set a new two-wheel record in 36.60sec. It had been a wonderful record-breaking 60th anniversary meeting and, among the various parades, the huge ex-Ernest Eldridge Fiat, which took the World Land Speed Record in 1924 at 145.9mph, rumbled up the hill in 49.01sec.

And, while the bigger single-seaters had definitely arrived in hillclimbing, the 1961 championship fell – for the last time – to the driver of an 1100 Cooper-JAP. This was the forceful and courageous David Good, who'd enjoyed a brilliantly consistent season.

For 1962 Tony Marsh decided to circuit-race the

BRM in 1500cc F1 form, and build a new chassis to accommodate the 2500cc engine for hillclimbing – the first Marsh Special. He didn't enter for the June Shelsley because he was planning to be racing in the Monaco Grand Prix the same day. But his BRM wasn't ready, so he came to Shelsley and demonstrated the Marsh-BRM. The watches were running to catch the first sub-34 climb at 33.91, although of course as a demonstration it couldn't count as a record. The official winner was another Grand Prix BRM, Ray Fielding's ex-Dan Gurney car, which got very near the record with a 34.65sec. Chris Summers had forsaken the Farley Special for an equally hairy beast, an old F2 Cooper with 4.4-litre Chevrolet V8 engine – possibly the first sighting of the type of English chassis/American motor single-seater that would become common on the hills, and the circuits, before the decade was out. The Cooper-Chev set second BTD in 34.80sec, just ahead of Phillips and the Fairley. Josh Randles' impressive 36.09sec with the 2-litre Cooper Monaco was a new sports car record, 0.61sec ahead of Scragg, and was the fourth fastest climb of the day.

Ian McLaughlin, whose yellow Cooper-JAP had been picking up points in the championship rounds, set BTD in the July inter-club team event although, as the programme finished early, extra unofficial runs were offered, and Bryan Eccles' Cooper-JAP went up even quicker, in 35.32sec, actually quicker than the old Boshier-Jones record. Eccles would become a serious championship contender in future years.

At the August meeting, for only the third time

Phil Scragg's Lister-Jaguar was based on the Ecurie Ecosse Monzanapolis circuit car.

George Brown's Vincent rockets off the line. This is the damp August 1963 meeting, but two years earlier George lowered the two-wheel record to 36.6sec.

in Shelsley history, BTD was set by a motorcycle. The rider was of course the irrepressible George Brown, and he and his Vincent were helped by the weather, for his 36.82sec was set in the dry. The sports-racers ran on a dry hill too. Peter Boshier-Jones, who'd replaced his Lola with a Climax-powered Lotus 23, and Phil Scragg in the Lister both climbed in 37.24sec, which was to remain joint four-wheeled BTD. Then the rain came, providing a wonderful test of skill for the championship runners. Having written off his Special in a big accident at Rest & Be Thankful, Marsh had the BRM engine back in its original chassis and garnered 10 points by 0.46sec from the brave Summers. Third place was another V8-engined Cooper, this time using 2.5-litre Daimler power. At the wheel was a bearded young Surrey engineer called Peter Westbury, who would go on to become a major force in hillclimbing within a

few months. In the class runs, when the rain was at its worst, Westbury beat all the rest of the big single-seaters, Marsh included, but by the championship run-offs the track was cleaner and Westbury's less powerful car was at a disadvantage.

The 1962 championship went to Arthur Owen, who used an ex-Formula 1 Cooper-Climax, but 1963 would be the first year since Sydney Allard's 1949 season that the title would go to a car specifically built for hillclimbing. This was Peter Westbury's pale metallic blue Felday, which used his faithful Daimler engine, now supercharged, in a heavily modified Lotus 22 frame with a far more upright seating position, which Westbury felt would better suit the task of rushing up narrow twisty hills. Tony Marsh built another Special, a very light car with 1500cc supercharged Climax power, but for the June Shelsley he was back with the faithful BRM. Now he could officially leave the

record in the 33sec bracket with a 33.54.

Peter Boshier-Jones had graduated to a single-seater Lotus 22 chassis for his supercharged Climax engine, and set second fastest time in the championship runs before depositing enough oil on the hill to reduce times for the rest of the day. The Felday broke its transmission, so Westbury borrowed David Good's now Daimler-engined Cooper, but joint third-place points went to Ray Fielding's 2.2 Lotus-Climax and Phil Scragg, untypically using a single-seater BRM while he waited for his latest wild sports car to be finished: an American Chaparral. Patsy Burt's long-standing ladies' record fell to a determined Scot, Agnes Mickel, in her husband's smart red 2.5 Cooper, the ex-Arthur Owen championship-winning car. For the traditionalists among the spectators, the high point of the day was a pair of runs by a Shelsley Special of yore. John Bolster had been

encouraged to extract *Bloody Mary* from her resting place in the National Motor Museum at Beaulieu, and attacked the hill with all his old hectic verve, elbows akimbo. His two runs were officially demonstrations, but the clocks were running, and his times were only 2sec off the old girl's best effort of 15 years earlier.

The now-familiar July inter-club meeting attracted 29 three-car teams, with the Liverpool MC winning on handicap with a mix of Lotus 23, Mini-Cooper and Jaguar 3.8. Not surprisingly the Midland AC home team of George Keylock's Cooper-Buick, Ray Terry's Lotus 7-Climax and Tony Griffiths' Lotus 18 was heavily handicapped. The extraordinary variety among the various teams included Welshman Charlie Sgonina in the ex-Jim Clark/Border Reivers Aston Martin DBR1, which he'd driven on the road from Wales; Ralph Broad in one of his own Broadspeed Mini-Coopers

Before building the first Felday, Peter Westbury used this V8 Daimler-powered Cooper with four open exhausts each side.

Huge SU carb and Shorrock supercharger sit atop the Climax engine in Peter Boshier-Jones' very effective Lotus 22 hillclimber.

– he was beaten by Ashley Cleave's venerable but always rapid Morris – and championship contender Peter Boshier-Jones, who set individual BTD with a useful 34.57. These well-subscribed inter-club events recall a time when local clubs were the backbone of British motorsport. Today, with very notable exceptions like the MAC, there are few strong area clubs that have active competition memberships.

Pete Bosh was on top again in the August championship round. Westbury was absent and Marsh, having sold the BRM, was back in the little Special, now with 2-litre Climax power. But on a damp day the yellow supercharged Lotus and its driver's smooth, unflustered style made the Welshman uncatchable. David Good's Cooper-Daimler beat Marsh into second place. Despite the

tricky conditions, one of the stars of the day was the venerable pairing of Davenport and *Spider*, whose hairy and crowd-pleasing 45.27sec climb was only 4.6 seconds slower than Marsh! During practice Chris Summers lost control of the Cooper-Chevrolet after the finishing line and spun into several cars in the top paddock waiting to return down the hill.

For 1964 another new factor was to make its presence felt: four-wheel-drive. It had been tried before in hillclimbing, but the Ferguson P99 was a four-wheel-drive Grand Prix car, which had won a race at Oulton Park in Stirling Moss' hands, and done a continental mountain hillclimb at Ollons-Villars driven by Jo Bonnier. Ferguson Research lent the car to Peter Westbury for a concerted, and victorious, attack on the British Hillclimb

Championship, although he missed both Shelsley rounds. The June meeting was another Boshier-Jones benefit. With a flawlessly smooth run in 33.35sec, Peter took 0.19sec off Marsh's hill record to put his family name back on the roll of honour. Marsh discovered a broken chassis tube on the Marsh-Climax so confined himself to one run, which was good enough for second BTD ahead of Ray Fielding's Lotus 21 and John Macklin, who had managed to squeeze one of the comparatively light all-alloy 3.5-litre Buick V8s into the back of a Formula Junior Cooper. This versatile engine, used by Rover in long generations of saloons and four-by-fours, was to play a substantial role in hillclimbing. Meanwhile, battle continued between Patsy Burt and Agnes Mickel. Both lowered the ladies' record, with Agnes taking it back to Scotland by 0.1sec.

The July inter-club meeting mirrored the previous year's, with a mix of Walton-Bristol, Allard J1 and Ford Cortina making up the winning North Midland MC team, and Peter Boshier-Jones taking individual BTD in 33.99sec. And Pete Bosh set his fifth consecutive Shelsley BTD at the August meeting with a 33.76 climb. Marsh set second BTD 0.09sec slower, but in the championship runs, with the hill now very oily, he couldn't break into the 34s. But he was still second quickest ahead of Macklin and Peter Meldrum, also using a supercharged Lotus 22 but with Ford power. In other classes, the motorcyclists returned so that George Brown – who else? – could break his own two-wheel Shelsley record in 36.28sec, crossing the finish line at 107mph; and John Horrex took his Cooper-Norton Mk9 up faster than a 500 had ever been, in 38.54sec. Phil Scragg had given up

Ashley Cleave's neat road-going Morris was faster than it looked, and over many decades it humbled a lot of much more glamorous machinery.

Grace, space and pace in hillclimbing: Bob Jennings' immaculate Jaguar 3.8 was always stylishly driven and very fast.

on the troublesome Chaparral project and was now busy with a Lightweight E-type Jaguar, setting a new class record in 37.35sec. In the vintage class, Ronald "Steady" Barker climbed in the Napier with which C.A. Bird competed at Shelsley in 1911.

For 1965 Tony Marsh took a long look at the Marsh Special and decided it needed more horsepower and better handling. The extra power came from one of the light-alloy Buick V8s, and longer wheelbase and wider track made the car much more stable. In many ways this was a forerunner of a whole new generation of hillclimb challengers. In Marsh's hands it was devastatingly fast straight away, and in June Tony helped the Midland AC to celebrate Shelsley Walsh's 60th anniversary with the first sub-33 record. Reported *Motoring News*:

Tony Marsh was magnificent. Having already set a new record with a perfectly adequate 33.16, he came to the line for the final timed climb of the day with nothing to lose. A perfectly controlled start projected the newly re-crowned King of Shelsley up the hill to break the record once again, leaving the figure at an untouchable 32.94 seconds.

Peter Boshier-Jones broke his transmission on the Lotus 22, so Peter Meldrum's 22 was second from Macklin and Tony Griffiths in the ex-Marsh BRM. Peter Westbury, having returned the Ferguson P99 to its owners, demonstrated the unique, and unraced, BRM 670P four-wheel-drive F1 car. He'd wanted to compete with it, but BRM boss Sir Alfred Owen, a strictly religious man, would not allow BRMs to be raced in this country on Sundays: Westbury was said to have climbed in 33.03 in practice, which can't have been lost on Tony Marsh. Patsy Burt's immaculate pale blue Cooper-Climax was fast enough to be sixth in the championship run-offs, and get her Ladies' Record back with 35.81sec. Harry Ratcliffe turned up with

a wild Mini – it had a V8 Buick engine in the back, driving the front wheels, and not surprisingly suffered from traction problems – and the Elton family, father Tom and son Spencer, both won their classes in 1100 Cooper-JAP and 500 Cooper-Norton. Among the Diamond Jubilee demonstrations was one by Alan Warner's 1910 Lanchester, which had a very spry George Lanchester in the passenger seat. He, more than anyone, must have been able to see how Shelsley had changed and developed since that first meeting in 1905.

The July meeting was no longer an inter-club team handicap affair, but allowed MAC committee member and future president Tony Griffiths to set his first Shelsley BTD with the BRM in 34.90sec in the absence of most of the other front-runners. But they were all there for the August championship round. There were a few slippery patches after morning rain, but Marsh's BTD in 33.50sec clinched the 1965 title – his first for eight

years. The hard-trying Macklin set second BTD, but in the championship runs he was beaten by Boshier-Jones. After Meldrum hit the bank at the Esses, Bristolian Ian Swift was next up, with a 4.7-litre Ford V8 powering his Cooper.

The pattern was the same at the June 1966 meeting: Marsh quickest, from Boshier-Jones and an impressive Meldrum, who was quickest of all during the class runs. The MAC had even more work to do than usual before the meeting took place. The previous week there was a landslip at The Crossing and earth-moving equipment, hired to clear the road, had left clay and earth on the surface. Then it rained, so times were slow all weekend. The non-championship July event was won by a new name, Birmingham baker Mike Hawley, with a twin-cam Brabham BT16. Hawley shone against stronger opposition in the torrentially wet August, setting a surprise BTD with a brilliant 40.17 ahead of Marsh and Boshier-Jones. "Rain very nearly stopped play", reported

June 1967, and a determined Tony Marsh rockets up the hill in the now-4wd Marsh Special to a new outright record, 1.7sec under the old one.

Autosport. "The meeting was halted for nearly an hour while streams of water coursed down the hill." Phil Scragg was fourth in the championship runs in yet another new sports-racer toy, a 4.7-litre Ford V8-powered Lola T70, originally intended for CanAm racing rather than hillclimbing.

Marsh had taken the championship again, and now his goal was to complete a second trio of titles to match those in 1955, 1956 and 1957. But the competition was getting ever fiercer, and in 1966 he'd won fewer than half the rounds, so over the winter he plotted a big step forward with the Marsh Special. After quietly studying the Ferguson and the BRM 670P in action, he noted that four-wheel-drive gave tremendous traction off the line and out of slow corners but, in the corners themselves, time seemed to be lost in wheel-scrub. So he dreamed up a simple sprag-gear device whereby the Marsh's front wheels were powered when the car was running in a straight line, but could be switched to freewheel in corners. A new chassis was built up, using many parts from the old car, and ran initially in 2wd form until the new transmission parts were ready. Thus the new car made its 4wd debut at the June 1967 meeting, on what was to prove a historic day. Tony Marsh chopped the huge margin of 1.71 seconds off the hill record.

Part of the credit for this, in fact, had to go to Shelsley's superb new layer of tarmac, for the hill had been completely resurfaced over the winter. Helped by fine weather, no fewer than 62 climbs were made under their existing class records. Marsh's strongest challenge came from Midlander Bryan Eccles, who had a compact Brabham BT14 single-seater into which a light-alloy Oldsmobile V8 had been squeezed. He was only 0.32sec slower than Marsh, while a terrific performance from Patsy Burt in her new McLaren-Oldsmobile single-seater gave her a richly deserved third place as well a conclusive new ladies' record.

Records fell in almost every other class, including a storming 33.27 sports car record for Phil Scragg's Lola T70. Following his earlier strategy with the HWM and Lister, Scragg had replaced the streamlined bodywork with a homely cycle-winged effort which made the car look like an overgrown Lotus 7 but gave much better visibility on the hills. In typical Scragg style, this formidable weapon was road-registered. David Good had persuaded Sir Alfred Owen to sell him the 4wd BRM and was having a strong season with it, although at Shelsley he nudged the bank and finished well down.

But Bryan Eccles was clearly the man after Tony Marsh's Shelsley crown. While most of the

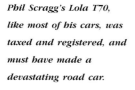

Phil Scragg's Lola T70, like most of his cars, was taxed and registered, and must have made a devastating road car.

championship contenders were absent he took the Brabham-Olds to the July members' meeting and, in perfect conditions, broke the hill record with the first-ever sub-31sec climb, managing 30.83sec. In August he was almost as quick with a 30.98, earning 10 championship points ahead of Tony Marsh, whose Special had an incipient misfire and was 0.17sec slower. Mike Hawley, now using 2-litre Climax power in his latest Brabham, was third ahead of a lad from Knaresborough, Peter Lawson, with a twin-cam Brabham. Once more the big V8 sports-racers provided great entertainment, with a fine joust for the new class record between Bob Rose (4.7 McLaren) and Ray

Terry (3.8 Elva-Buick). The class lead seesawed between them until Terry ended up with a best of 32.58sec. But Rose was certainly trying hard in the big CanAm McLaren, "no doubt needled", surmised *Motoring News*, "by having been followed all the way from Worcester into the paddock that morning by a policeman in a Minivan, who couldn't believe such a machine could legally be driven on the road".

Having completed his second trio of titles – but this time only narrowly from Eccles – Marsh returned for 1968, although he announced that pressures of work would not allow him to do a full season. Eccles was planning a new 4wd car

Peter Lawson beat Tony Marsh in June 1968 to score his first Shelsley BTD and points towards his championship title. This is the unique BRM 670P four-wheel-drive Formula 1 car.

Ray Terry's Elva, with alloy V8 Buick engine and four-wheel-drive, was a ferociously effective sports-racer on the hills.

(which never appeared), while David Good had sold the 4wd BRM to young Peter Lawson.

The June meeting was one of those perfect Shelsley occasions, with superb weather, and stirring battles all down the programme. There was a fascinating variety of machinery, from Bill Needham's shrieking twin-cam Mini and John Macklin's 7-litre Cobra to Jack Richards' Type 51 Bugatti and the irrepressible Basil Davenport, still going strong in *Spider*. Lawson, already familiar with the BRM, was 0.19sec off the record, but he still beat Marsh by a clear 0.43sec. Although nobody knew it at the time, this was to be Tony's last appearance at a hillclimb for nearly 20 years. Berkshire baronet Sir Nick Williamson was becoming increasingly rapid with his twin-cam Brabham, and set third BTD ahead of Geoff Rollason's FVA-powered Lotus 41.

It had become the custom for the Shelsley team to insure against rain, which always had a dramatic

effect on spectator takings. For the purposes of any claim, a small bottle was placed at the top of the hill to measure actual precipitation. The July members' meeting was the first time since the MAC had started investing in Pluvius Insurance that a claim was made, although by the afternoon the rain had stopped. Bespectacled businessman Martin Brain, who had forsaken his earlier Daimler-powered Cooper for an ex-Jochen Rindt F1 Cooper chassis powered by a huge 7.2-litre Chrysler V8, took BTD in 36.40sec from Rollason.

Lawson was fastest again in August in 31.37sec. It rained before the championship runs, in which Lawson was streets ahead of everyone else: without the challenge of Tony Marsh, he already had the 1968 title in the bag. An intriguing second in the run-offs was Ray Terry's Elva-Buick, which had been adapted to run Marsh-type 4wd by race engineer Chas Beattie. Tony Griffiths, who'd had an unhappy period with a purpose-built 2wd

Felday, was now much more comfortable in a straightforward Brabham twin-cam and was third ahead of a driver who would become a pillar of Shelsley: Roy Lane. Roy had graduated from smaller single-seaters to an orange Brabham with alloy V8 Buick/Olds engine and was now a serious championship contender – as he would continue to be for more than 35 years.

Four-wheel-drive was the thing to have, and Yorkshireman David Hepworth had built up a Chevrolet-powered single-seater around Brabham bits, which was very effective. He took BTD at the June 1969 Shelsley, 0.37sec adrift of the record but ahead of Jim Johnstone in the ex-Roy Lane Brabham, and Roy himself in his new self-built Brabham-based car, the TechCraft-Buick. An interesting departure from the pushrod American V8 route, presaging the F1-derived sophistication to come, was the Brabham with V8 four-cam Climax engine shared by Mike MacDowel and Bob Jennings. It lacked the ultimate grunt to do better than sixth, but MacDowel, whose 1950s racing career had briefly got as far as Formula 1 before

being cut short by an accident, was catching the hillclimbing bug in a big way.

Another to go the 4wd route was Peter Blankstone, whose Marsh system Brabham-Olds V8 won the July members' meeting. But at the August championship round there was a new BTD name, and a new hill record – with a two-wheel-drive car. Shelsley Walsh has always been a power and torque hill, and Martin Brain's mighty 7.2-litre Cooper-Chrysler shaved 0.11sec off Eccles' record with a rumbling 30.72. Roy Lane's 31.51 was a best yet for him and good enough for second place, while Tony Griffiths shared the Cooper-Chrysler to take third ahead of John Cussins in the ex-Lawson 4wd BRM. Hepworth was absent, having crashed his car the week before, but he had still done enough to end the year as Hillclimb Champion.

An important innovation for 1970 was a new season-long contest to run alongside the main British Hillclimb series. Called the Leaders' Championship and sponsored – as was the main series at this time – by Shell, it was open to all non-

Martin Brain's 7.2-litre Chrysler-powered Cooper had the biggest engine of any Shelsley winner since Edwardian times, and took the record in 1969.

championship contenders at each championship round, awarding points for positions in each class.

The familiar Shelsley surroundings looked very different as the cars and trailers arrived for the June 1970 meeting. The paddock, "always either a dust-bowl or a mud-bath", as *Autosport* put it, had been properly hard-surfaced for the first time. Also, the braking area at the top of the hill was now extended, a source of relief to several drivers of the faster cars who often found the most exciting part of the climb was getting stopped after crossing the finish line. David Hepworth set fastest time in the class runs, but then sportingly lent his car to Peter Blankstone, whose Brabham had engine trouble. In Blankstone's hands the Hepworth broke its transmission, leaving the way clear for Nick Williamson's latest charger, a full-house Formula 5000 McLaren M10A/B, which equalled Martin Brain's record en route to 10 championship points and BTD. Brain wasn't there to defend his record: tragically an accident at a Silverstone race meeting had cost him his life. David Good also had an F5000 McLaren now and was 0.15sec slower than Williamson, chased by Tony Griffiths, the incumbent chairman of the MAC, in his Brabham-FVA. Roy Lane and John Cussins had swapped cars, Cussins getting the TechCraft and Roy the remains of the 4wd BRM which Cussins had crashed heavily at Prescott. Roy

incorporated most of the bits into his new car, the TechCraft-BRM.

The July meeting had a different format this year, with Saturday's event co-promoted with the VSCC. It was won by Tony Griffiths, but with Jonty Williamson hustling his 1923 V12 Delage up the hill to fastest pre-war time. On Sunday Roy Lane took his first Shelsley BTD with the TechCraft-BRM in a rousing 30.87sec. Meanwhile the entire championship season had become a battle between Hepworth and Williamson, and at Shelsley in August – in the presence of the Lord Mayor of Birmingham, no less – Hepworth got a maximum 11 points by taking 0.23sec off the hill record. The always-brave David Good dramatically rolled his McLaren at the Esses but was unhurt, and Williamson was runner-up. At the end of the season Williamson and Hepworth tied on nett points, with the baronet taking the title by virtue of more dropped points. The first Leaders' Champion was Gloucestershire architect Chris Cramer, whose storming 35.34sec climb at the July meeting in his lightweight 1328cc Mini stood for many years as the fastest saloon climb of Shelsley.

Not many years before, the idea of ascending Shelsley Walsh in under half a minute had seemed pure fantasy, but it was clear that the goal was creeping nearer. It was David Hepworth who did it first, in his home-brewed 4wd car, on 13 June 1971.

Its four fuel-injection trumpets gulping in good Worcestershire air, Chris Cramer's ultra-light 1328cc Mini sets a new saloon record in July 1970.

It came as the climax of a dramatic day, after Hepworth had shaved his own record by 0.09sec during the class runs, and by another 0.25 on his first championship run. When almost everyone else was upsizing, reigning champ Williamson had gone down to an 1800cc FVA in his new Brabham, and he also got under the old record with 30.26sec. Then Tony Griffiths took his new Brabham BT35X, with five-litre Repco engine, up in a superb 30.08. But he held the record for barely a minute before, on the very last run of the meeting, Hepworth wrote another page of the Shelsley history book with his 29.92sec effort. It was described by hillclimb historian and pundit Chris Mason as "an awesome, scrabbling, over-revving climb, with Hepworth appearing to bully his protesting car to the top".

There was another double restricted meeting in July. In Saturday's joint MAC/VSCC promotion Tony Griffiths was fastest on the Saturday, with David Kergon's ERA *Hanuman* the fastest pre-war

car. Roy Lane, who had dispensed with the TechCraft-BRM in favour of an F5000 McLaren M10B, was fastest on Sunday. In August nobody except Hepworth could get below the half-minute, but the Yorkshireman took another 0.28sec off his own record. Mike MacDowel's latest mount was a Palliser, like Griffiths using a 5-litre Repco V8 power unit, and he was second from Lane, Griffiths and Williamson. The speed trap at the top of the hill caught Griffiths at 121mph over the finish line, appreciably faster than anyone else. The season ended with Hepworth as the deserving British Hillclimb Champion, while the Leaders' Champion was Tony Bancroft, a consistently fast Yorkshireman whose hairy TVR Tuscan was conducted under various pseudonyms such as Spotty Muldoon and Spotty Smith, to avoid parental disapproval. At the June meeting he took the sports car record down to 35.83sec.

Roy Lane finally got his first National meeting BTD in June 1972, using a new ex-F1 McLaren

David Good's short right arm never slowed him at all. At the June 1970 meeting his F5000 McLaren was 0.15sec off BTD, pipped by Nick Williamson's similar car.

chassis, after Hepworth was slowed by a dud battery during the class runs. Then it rained, and Hepworth's 4wd put him 2sec clear of everybody on the run-offs, with Lane runner-up. Nick Williamson was third with his latest pursuit of the smaller car theme, a 2-litre Cosworth BDA-powered March: he was to go on to be champion again that year. The July VSCC co-promotion brought out the usual variety, from Denis Jenkinson in an ex-Le Mans Lagonda and Hamish Moffat and Patrick Marsh in ERAs to, of course, Basil Davenport, 48 years on from his first Shelsley. Tony Griffiths took Saturday's BTD and Mike Hawley Sunday's after Lane crashed the McLaren in practice.

After the August meeting there was a new name in the list of Shelsley record-holders. Mike MacDowel had swapped the difficult Palliser chassis for a Brabham and, using the same Repco engine, took a big chunk off Hepworth's target with an aggressive yet stylishly tidy 29.29sec climb. Also below the half-minute that day were Lane (29.77) and Richard Thwaites, in the ex-Good McLaren. Fine battles in the classes included the sports-racers, with Tony Bancroft (3.0 Chevron), David Good (1.8 Martin), Tony Harrison (7.0 McLaren) and Reg Phillips (1.8 Chevron), all covered by 0.13sec.

MacDowel was determined that 1973 would be his championship year, and he did it with some ease. His performances at the two Shelsley rounds were brilliant: BTD and a new hill record at both.

VIP visitors in 1973: Raymond Mays (right), debonair at 74, ponders the fall of the 29-second barrier with supercharger king Chris Shorrock.

In June the 29sec barrier was toppled with a 28.82, helped by some new Firestone B36 slick tyres. Nick Williamson had got Lyncar to modify his F2 March to accommodate an F1 Cosworth DFV engine, calling the resulting confection the Marlyn, and he was second, just 0.08sec away from getting into the 28s, with the McLarens of Thwaites and Lane next. In August Thwaites produced a 28.55, and this was just the spur that MacDowel needed. Magically he found a little bit more, to leave the record at 28.21sec. Williamson and Griffiths, who was also using DFV power now, were next up.

The restricted meeting in July was now treated as useful practice by the serious hillclimbers, with Chris Cramer's 2-litre March setting BTD on Saturday and MacDowel slipping in a quiet 29.09 on Sunday. The lease at that time still only allowed six days' activity on the hill per year, but the non-championship meetings were growing in stature, paving the way for the time when Shelsley would have meetings every month from May to September. At the August meeting Gerry Flewitt bowed out as MAC secretary after 15 years at the helm, to be replaced by Steve Perry.

The June 1974 meeting was another memorable one. This was for less pleasant reasons because showers kept the hill damp for much of the afternoon, and for more pleasant ones because of two presentations made to long-time stalwarts of hillclimbing. One award went to the evergreen Basil Davenport, who had clocked up half a century at Shelsley, and assaulted the hill with his usual no-nonsense vigour. The other went to Ashley Cleave, the West Countryman who had finally retired after being a permanent fixture at events all over Britain. Ashley's car was a humble, standard looking, but carefully developed, 1937 Morris 8 two-seater, in which he drove great distances to meetings from his home in Cornwall and regularly posted remarkably quick times, frequently winning his class through the 1950s and 1960s against far more glamorous machinery. Topping the championship climbs was MacDowel again, from Williamson, Cramer and Lane, who had replaced the McLaren with a more compact McRae F5000 chassis.

At the restricted July weekend Ken MacMaster set BTD both days in his nimble GRD 1600 Hart-powered single-seater, an interesting pointer to the next change in fashion for Hillclimb Championship contenders. The fastest pre-war car

over the VSCC Saturday was Guy Smith's single-seater Frazer Nash.

MacDowel was again top scorer in August, giving him his fifth consecutive National Shelsley BTD and taking him further towards his second championship title. At the prize-giving this courteous man, who now had so many hillclimb victories under his belt, spoke with quiet emotion about how much more a BTD meant at the historic Worcestershire venue than anywhere else. But he was 0.4sec off his own record on this occasion, and the ever-improving Roy Lane was a scant 0.05 sec slower, with Nick Williamson third in the Marlyn-DFV. As always, the other classes were full of interest. Sussex violin restorer Peter Voigt took an extraordinary four seconds off the old 500cc racing car record with his Voigt-Renwick Special, powered by a flat-four Konig two-stroke

marine engine, climbing in 33.44sec. And Scotsman John Cleland, later to become a leading touring car racer, set a new sports car record with his Chevron B19 in 30.21sec. The half-minute sports car time was now beckoning.

At the June 1975 meeting Shelsley Walsh celebrated its 70th birthday in style. Raymond Mays and Whitney Straight were among the spectators, and Basil Davenport was out with *Spider*, of course. Roy Lane and his McRae were proving to be the dominant force this season, and he set BTD, chased by Chris Cramer's March-Hart and the rapidly improving Alister Douglas-Osborn, who had graduated from a fast U2 to a 2-litre Brabham, much modified by Lincolnshire chassis man Mike Pilbeam. Both Pilbeam and "ADO" were to play a major role in hillclimbing in the seasons to come, and Alister in particular was to become a real star

Basil Davenport celebrated half a century of hillclimbing at Shelsley in 1974 by attacking the hill in Spider with all his old vigour.

of Shelsley. Three weeks later, at the restricted weekend, he was fastest on both days in Lane's absence, but Roy was back on top for the August championship meeting. In practice he did the first ever sub-28 climb, and in the event itself he left the record at 28.03sec, clinching his first championship title as he did so. It had been a perfect season for Roy, with an astonishing 11 BTDs, 10 of them consecutively. Douglas-Osborn and Cramer once again supplied the closest competition.

Come 1976 there was increasing sophistication among the front-running hillclimbers. While Roy Lane remained happy with pushrod American V8 power, Douglas-Osborn now had a Cosworth DFV F1 engine in a new Pilbeam chassis, and Chris Cramer was using a 3.4-litre Cosworth V6 in a new March. Alister soon proved to be one of the best hillclimb talents of all. He was to hold the hill record uninterruptedly – apart from a one-year interregnum by Martyn Griffiths – for 14 years. It was ADO who was the first to duck below 28 seconds with a new 27.92 record in June: in the championship runs he was fractionally slower, but still bested Lane by just six thousandths of a second. Next up were Cramer and Williamson who, after a year off, was back with his old Cosworth DFV in a 1974 F1 March chassis.

The July non-championship weekend had continued to gain status, both because the championship contenders could use it for valuable practice and because it was easier for the lesser lights to get their entries accepted. Run as two separate one-day meetings, it provided a round of the BARC (British Automobile Racing Club) Hillclimb Championship as well. Douglas-Osborn achieved a sensational 27.12sec in practice with the Pilbeam-DFV and set BTD on Saturday. On Sunday his final run looked quicker still. But, most unusually, the timing gear malfunctioned. He returned to the start, reported *Autosport*, looking a bit like a thunderstorm about to happen, and was given another run, but understandably he was now somewhat unsettled and it looked a little wild. But it was still a new record, another 0.28sec under his previous mark at 27.64. Roy Lane hit the bank with the McRae, and it was Cramer who ended up second fastest. For the August meeting, therefore, ADO had something to aim for, and the result was yet another record in 27.39sec, with Lane and Cramer the bridesmaids once more, both of them under 28 seconds. At the end of the season Lane and Douglas-Osborn tied at the top of the championship table but, taking dropped points into account, the title was Lane's.

Josh Sadler was one of several Porsche exponents in the 1970s with his Autofarm 911.

Martyn Griffiths, having graduated to single-seaters from a U2 clubman's car, now had his 2.2-litre March-Hart tweaked for hillclimbing by Mike Pilbeam, and at the June 1977 meeting he set his first Shelsley BTD. Dreadful rain during practice turned the finish paddock into a quagmire, but the resourceful MAC got a contractor in who worked through the night laying hardcore to make it usable and washing the mud off the top portion of the hill. Most of the event itself was dry, but the rain returned after the first championship runs, at which point Chris Cramer and ADO were second and third. The 1600cc sports-racing class was won by the U2 of a third Boshier-Jones brother, Anthony.

At the July non-championship meeting ADO

Roy Lane dominated the 1975 championship with his McRae, and in August left the Shelsley record at 28.03sec.

Mike MacDowel won back-to-back championships with the beautiful Brabham-Repco BT36X, bringing the record down to 28.21sec in 1973.

was back in control, shaving a further four-hundredths off his own hill record, ahead of Cramer and Griffiths. In August the weather was dreadful, but that didn't keep away 7000 hardy spectators. The road was getting a little dryer as Douglas-Osborn slithered and skated up the hill on the edge of control to take a BTD that was a fat 1.19sec ahead of second man Roy Lane, who now had the ex-Nick Williamson F1 March. This dominating performance helped to clinch ADO's only championship title – although he would go on setting Shelsley BTDs for another decade.

After the August 1977 meeting Steve Perry retired as MAC secretary, to be replaced by Mark Joseland, a chartered surveyor with a taste for vintage Frazer Nashes. He was to hold the post for a dedicated 22 years, longer than anyone except Leslie Wilson. Since he retired in 1999 his service to Shelsley has continued in the role of club archivist.

The 1978 season brought another new star in the shape of Bristol garage owner David Franklin, who put his faith in a BMW-powered F2 March. ADO took much of the season getting his brand new Pilbeam-DFV MP31 to handle as well as his old R22, while Mike MacDowel, despite various efforts to retire, was back again with an F3 Ralt, extended by Derek Gardner of Tyrrell to take a 3.3-litre Cosworth DFV. The result was called the Coogar, taking the first three letters of MacDowel's business (Jaguar dealers Coombs of Guildford) and Gardner's name. The June meeting was officially the 100th National Shelsley event, and Franklin's little red and white March took BTD by 0.14sec from MacDowel, with Griffiths third. MacDowel was a popular winner in July, from Cramer and ADO, while in August the four-cylinder cars were again setting the pace. Franklin did a 27.71 nearly at the end of the day and Griffiths, trying to beat it, clouted the bank coming out of the Top Ess hard enough to ruin his run. His earlier run still gave him second, from Cramer and MacDowel. Franklin ended the season as champion, by just one point from Griffiths. This talented and versatile driver did part-seasons in the championship series for a few more years and then graduated to historic racing on the circuits. More than 20 years later he is still one of the most respected exponents of this discipline.

At the end of 1978 an additional meeting was run in early October to raise money to restore the

Shelsley Walsh church, St Andrew's. It was a relaxed fun event, with drivers' wives taking part in tow cars and friends trying out each others' cars. BTD was set by Peter Kaye's Pilbeam, and a lot of money was raised in a good cause. Then during the winter the whole venue received a major upgrade. The hill was entirely resurfaced,

which removed several of the worst bumps. A new building in the paddock comprised his'n'hers flush toilets, washbasins with running water and even (compact) changing facilities, replacing the sheds with primitive chemical closets that had been there as long as anyone could remember. For the spectators there were improved pathways to access the viewing terraces at the Esses, and the PA system was upgraded. Perhaps the new surface was still settling in at the June meeting, for Martyn Griffiths failed by three-hundredths of a second to take Douglas-Osborn's two-year-old record. However he scored a clean sweep of BTDs at the three 1979 Shelsleys, in a season which saw

him win his first British Hillclimb Championship title after being runner-up for the previous two years. ADO was 0.04sec slower than Martyn in June, and 0.18sec slower in August. Roy Lane experimented with a fascinating March F1 variant, the unraced six-wheel "4-6-0" with pairs of back wheels in tandem, but it didn't work as well as he'd hoped. After failing to qualify for the June championship runs the car was converted back to a four-wheeler.

By now hillclimbing was established as a specialist sport that demanded its own focus. Chassis designers of the calibre of Mike Pilbeam, Ron Tauranac of Ralt and Robin Herd of March were prepared to build or adapt cars specifically for the hills. While drivers still moved on from hillclimbing to circuit racing – David Franklin, for one – it was very rare for a circuit racer to go hillclimbing during a busy season, or vice versa. As there were 16 rounds in the RAC Hillclimb Championship, a full hillclimbing season left little room for anything else. With this specialisation had come a huge increase in sophistication, and in cost, for the type of car required for a serious tilt at BTD. In 1960 a Cooper-JAP was still capable of winning a championship round at Shelsley. By the end of the following decade it was Formula 1 engines and purpose-built chassis that were setting records.

But while the main focus was, as always, on the battles for outright BTD and championship points, there was still a lot of spectacular hillclimbing among the various classes. Often friendly fights would continue from meeting to meeting, such as the ongoing tussles between the well-developed Porsches of Tony Bancroft and Josh Sadler, and there was always stirring stuff among the smaller single-seaters – like the tiny 250cc Motus-Yamaha of Ray Rowan, effectively a streamlined kart with suspension, from which Rowan was to graduate to larger single-seaters. The clubman's cars were going ever faster – in 1980 Richard Jones would get well into the 28-second bracket in his 2-litre Hart-powered U2 – and some "silhouette" saloons were starting to appear, full-blooded spaceframe racing cars cloaked in lightweight shells that approximated to the shape of a humble small saloon. At all levels, hillclimbing was healthy, and if it was no longer as cheap as it had been to compete in the lesser classes, this was still infinitely more affordable than any form of circuit racing. The prospect for the 1980s looked good.

Alister Douglas-Osborn's long reign as the King of Shelsley began in 1975, but by 1976 he had this DFV-powered Pilbeam R22 which gave him six BTDs in two seasons.

SHELSLEY'S LADIES

The role of women in motorsport, like the role of women in everything else, has changed out of all recognition during the life of the Shelsley Walsh hillclimb. But from the very beginning there were ladies competing at Shelsley, even if initially they were treated rather patronisingly as light relief from the serious business of the men's climbs. Study of the results of meetings reveals the fastest time by a lady going back to 1905, although an official ladies' record wasn't listed until 1927. Down the years there have been some female hillclimbers of great talent and competitiveness, and often meetings have been enhanced by a real battle for the Ladies' Record. These days the British Women Racing Drivers' Club includes Shelsley on their list of point-scoring events, and in 2004 the ladies' record fell below 27 seconds at the hand of Sue Young.

Ninety-nine years earlier, Miss Larkins used a little 6hp Wolseley to climb Shelsley in the less than startling time of 267.9sec. The following year the redoubtable Dorothy Levitt managed a much more impressive 92.4sec in a 50hp Napier. She wrote in her diary that night: "Car nearly went over embankment owing to greasy state of road." Despite being described by a contemporary as "slight in stature, shy and almost timid", Miss Levitt was a courageous and determined competitor, and also turned her hand to long-distance trials and powerboat racing. She was a leading light in the Ladies' Automobile Club of Great Britain and Ireland, which by 1909 had 400 members and headquarters at Claridges, the London hotel. Her

Joy Rainey on the limit at Crossing in the 2.8 Pilbeam. She eventually got down to 28.32sec with this car.

Doris Chilton on the line in 1922 in her 15.9hp Arrol Johnston. Her passengers are ladies too.

ladies' time remained unbeaten for seven years, until Laura Starkey went 4sec faster in 1913 in her 12/16 Sunbeam.

Post-World War I, Lilian Roper managed a creditable 71.3 sec in her little 1500cc AC in 1923, and a year later the big 7.6-litre Peugeot of Olive Stewart-Menzies ascended in 66sec dead. The delightfully-named Winifred Pink was a frequent competitor in a succession of Aston Martins, and then a real Shelsley star emerged in the shape of May Cunliffe. In 1926 she clocked 58.2sec in her stripped, spartan 3-litre Bentley, and for the following year, the first in which the ladies' record was recognised, she added a supercharger. Her 53.4sec not only set the record but also earned her fourth BTD. In 1928 she used a 1924 2-litre Grand Prix Sunbeam and set third BTD, bringing her record down to 51.2sec. Tragically, she crashed this car at another event when her father was

acting as riding mechanic, and he was killed. She briefly returned to Shelsley in 1936 to drive Philip Jucker's Alta, but this was the very wet meeting when she crashed after the finish line, breaking her jaw.

The Cunliffe Sunbeam record remained unbeaten for three years, but women competitors were now very much part of the Shelsley scene – so much so that they became the traditional openers of the programme, as *The Motor* explained in its report of the July 1930 event:

The steep, wooded banks were almost invisible under a great multitude of spectators: a sea of faces, of pretty summer hats, of parasols, here and there a glimpse of some girl's vivid, dainty frock, or a gleam of sunlight on the shining silver badge of a policeman. Promptly at 1.30pm, the hour fixed for the start, came

ABOVE: Winifred Pink's Aston Martin comes to the line in 1923. Front passenger is Aston Martin boss Lionel Martin.

LEFT: Lilian Roper was fastest lady in 1923 with her enthusiastically-driven 1500cc AC.

ABOVE: Elsie "Bill" Wisdom hit 50 seconds dead in July 1931 with her supercharged Frazer Nash.

RIGHT: Bill Wisdom and proud husband Tommy in the Orchard Paddock after her 1931 record.

a sonorous voice from the announcer, telling us that the women competitors were, as an act of courtesy, to be allowed to make the first ascents.

Over the loudspeakers came a weird banshee-like wail. It was the supercharger of a Mercedes down there at the start. At the wheel, thinly disguised under the pseudonym of "Miss Wyndham", was the Hon. Dorothy Paget.

There is heavy irony in the description "thinly disguised", for Dorothy Paget was a very large lady, given to eating hearty meals in the middle of the night, and famous not only as a prolific racehorse owner but also as the money behind the Birkin blower Bentley project. The patronising tone continues:

Mrs E.R. Hall took her Bentley steadily,

changing gear skilfully . . . the stop light was glowing brightly on Mrs Raymond Gough's elegant MG, so that someone suggested that her brake was on. She recorded 83.2sec . . . Mrs Wisdom took the sharp steep S bend in as pretty a little skid as you could wish to see.

In fact Elsie "Bill" Wisdom, wife of journalist and racer Tommy Wisdom, was a regular Brooklands racer and was very quick in her black supercharged Frazer Nash. In 1931 she took May Cunliffe's record with a climb in 50 seconds dead. The May 1933 meeting lined up 16 ladies, including one Miss B.G. Reece, in white overalls, a monocle and a Frazer Nash, Miss P. Altham in Whitney Straight's black Bentley coupé, and photographer's daughter and successful rally driver Kitty Brunell, in her fiancé Ken Hutchison's Bugatti. Hutchison, who held the Donington lap record in this car, was in the passenger seat, and

had a lively ride as Kitty hit the bank at the Esses. Fastest was ex-motorcycle dirt track rider Fay Taylour in one of the new MG K3 Magnettes.

Bill Wisdom's record was beaten in September 1933 by Cynthia Sedgwick, also Frazer Nash mounted, who took two clear seconds off in 48.0sec. But the following June a beautiful girl called Barbara Skinner reduced that to 46.6sec in her little white Morris Minor special, much-modified, lightened and Zoller-supercharged by her father Carl Skinner of the SU (Skinners Union) carburettor firm.

This was followed by a long-running battle between Doreen Evans and Kay Petre. Doreen's brothers, Dennis and Kenneth Evans, ran Belle Vue Garage on Wandsworth Common, where Wilkie Wilkinson was responsible for engine tuning, and her single-seater blown R-type MG was very rapid. She took 1.2sec off the ladies' record in May 1935, but that September Kay Petre, a

May Cunliffe set three consecutive ladies' records. This is her first, in the 3-litre Bentley in 1926.

Fay Taylour was fastest of 16 ladies at the wet May 1933 Shelsley in this MG K3 Magnette.

slight, elegant girl of Canadian birth who was a fast Brooklands racer, appeared with the ex-Raymond Mays White Riley, now turned out in her favourite shade of pale blue. On her first run she shaved a fifth off the Doreen Evans mark. Doreen replied on her second run in the MG with 44.8 – only for Petre to equal that on her second attempt.

By now the crowd were cheering these two rather glamorous girls, and so, with a dead heat to resolve, the MAC decided to squeeze in a run-off at the end of the meeting to decide who should

take the record home. Doreen did not improve. Leaving her braking very late for the Esses, she got off-line and was slow through the Top Ess, so the result was merely a 46. Then Kay Petre jumped the start – but saw the red light, and was able to stop and reverse to the line to take her run again. No mistakes this time: the Riley flew up in 43.8sec, and the record was hers.

Petre continued with the Riley in 1936 and then switched to one of the supercharged Austin 7 single-seaters for 1937. In June she was pipped by

Cynthia Sedgwick's Frazer Nash was stripped down to take two seconds off Bill Wisdom's time in 1933.

FROM LEFT: Barbara Skinner, Doreen Evans, Kay Petre.

RIGHT: Doreen Evans in her R-type MG during her September 1935 duel with Kay Petre.

BELOW: Marjory Eccles is pushed to the start line in her Lagonda Rapier by ace tuner Robin Jackson (left) and husband Roy.

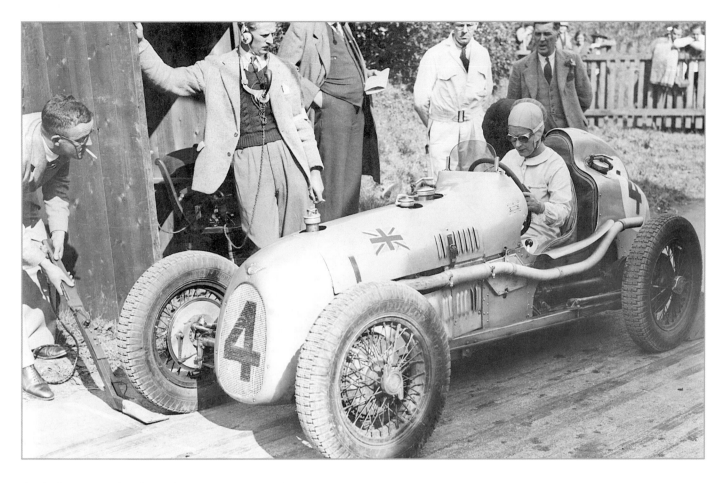

the little Morris of Barbara Skinner, now married to John Bolster, but in September, helped by the new timing to one-hundredth of a second, she shaved 0.02sec off her old record. At the same meeting Joan Richmond grappled with the front and rear engines of Robert Waddy's Fuzzi to be runner-up with an impressive 44.88sec – faster than Waddy himself.

In the final meeting before the war, Dorothy Stanley-Turner paid her first visit to Shelsley. Another circuit racer of note, she attributed her success entirely to a lucky elephant mascot given her by a well-wisher. Driving Bob Cowell's single-seater 1.5-litre Alta, she took the ladies' record in a rousing 43.40sec. Ironically, Cowell later underwent a sex-change operation to become Roberta Cowell, and took the ladies' record for herself 18 years later.

Many of the women drivers at Shelsley, then as now, have been wives and girlfriends having a go in their partner's car. In September 1948 Joan Gerard was one such, taking the helm of husband Bob's ERA R6B and slicing a fifth of a second off the pre-war record with a 43.18sec.

ABOVE: Kay Petre took her record back in 1937 with the supercharged Austin 7 single-seater.

LEFT: Dorothy Stanley-Turner took the ladies' record on her first visit to Shelsley in 1939, driving Bob Cowell's Alta.

ABOVE: Joan Gerard in her Riley Special in June 1948. Three months later, using one of her husband's ERAs, she broke the pre-war ladies' record.

RIGHT: Lady Mary Grosvenor, daughter of the Duke of Westminster, powers out of the Top Ess in her Grand Prix Alta, June 1950.

ABOVE: *Joy Cooke at the start of her September 1950 record run in Michael Christie's Kieft. The owner, looking anxious, is standing behind the car.*

LEFT: *Top rally driver Nancy Mitchell took the record in 1954 with this Cooper-JAP.*

ABOVE: Roberta Cowell comes to the line in the Emeryson-Alta before breaking the ladies' record in August 1957.

RIGHT: A fine shot of the stylish Pat Brock at the Esses in August 1959, climbing in 40.69sec.

ABOVE: Agnes Mickel (Cooper) wrested the ladies' record from Patsy Burt for two seasons.

LEFT: Patsy Burt's handling of the big McLaren M3A was always exemplary, and she held the ladies' record for 11 seasons with this car.

Margaret Blankstone shared husband Peter's U2 clubman's cars with great effect, and took the record in 1978.

Former record holders Patsy Burt and Margaret Blankstone compare notes in 1995. Bob Cooper listens.

With the advent of the Fifties and the near-supremacy of the 1100cc F3-based single-seaters, the ladies' record went the same way, with Joy Cooke's 43.16sec in Michael Christie's Kieft in 1950. Four years later the versatile Nancy Mitchell, who had built a fine reputation as a works rally driver, achieved 41.07sec in a works Cooper.

Patsy Burt started out riding horses and then got into rallying. Her demure expression hid a fierce competitiveness, and she was to have a long and successful motorsport career that encompassed hillclimbing, sprinting and record-breaking. At the August 1957 Shelsley her immaculate pale blue Cooper sports-racer took the ladies' record with 40.73sec – but only for a matter of minutes. Paul Emery's bulky Emeryson Grand Prix car, with a 2.5-litre Alta engine and shorn of its bodywork, went up 0.32sec faster with R. Cowell at the wheel. As Bob was now Roberta this, to Patsy's annoyance, stood as the new record. She got her own back the following year, with a single-seater 1500 Cooper-Climax, becoming the first lady to climb under 40sec and leaving the record at 38.66. She was also the first lady to score points in the RAC Hillclimb Championship, finishing eighth that day.

In 1959 Patsy finished a rousing fourth in the championship, with sixth at the June Shelsley and a further 1.03sec off the record, and that was to stand for four years. It finally fell to a bespectacled Scot called Agnes Mickel, who shared her husband Gray's ex-Arthur Owen 2.5-litre Cooper-Climax, and sometimes beat him. She clocked 36.30 in June 1963, and 35.87sec a year later. But in 1965 Patsy was back, now with a 2-litre Climax in a lighter Cooper, to sneak the record again by 0.06sec. Then she upgraded to a superb McLaren

single-seater, the M3A with 4.5-litre Oldsmobile V8 providing the horsepower, immaculately turned out in her usual pale blue colours. At the June 1967 meeting she set an immensely popular third BTD and took almost four whole seconds off her own record to leave this at 31.87sec, which put it out of reach for more than a decade. Her third place in the Hillclimb Championship run-off that day has never been equalled by a woman, before or since.

Patsy's record held until June 1978 when Margaret Blankstone, who shared a twin-cam 1600-powered U2 with husband Peter, shaved a fifth of a second off it in a very determined climb. But a year later there was another new name in the Ladies' Record book: Joy Rainey. Joy is an

Gillian Goldsmith (née Fortescue-Thomas) is the only lady to have set BTD at Shelsley, driving a V8 Anson single-seater, but she is more familiar in Terry Grainger's Lotus 23B.

FROM LEFT: Gillian Goldsmith, Sandra Tomlin, Sue Young.

inspiration to anyone who is physically different from the average. She is very small of stature, but in the cockpit she is talented, courageous, resourceful and hugely competitive. Joy held the Shelsley ladies' record, with a couple of brief interruptions, for 23 years, which is longer than anyone else in the hill's history. At first she used a neat clubman's car built by her engineer father,

Murray Rainey, and therefore called the Murrain, based on an old Dastle chassis with a Cosworth FVC engine which was eventually turbocharged. Joy wrestled this potent machine to a succession of records, gradually bringing her times down to 30.08sec.

In July 1980 Margaret Blankstone briefly took the record back by 0.04sec, but just five weeks later Joy pulled out all the stops to set the first sub-30 climb by a woman, in 29.75sec. The following year she did 29.36sec, and that stood for four more years until Gillian Fortescue-Thomas was offered some drives in Alan Payne's potent 4-litre V8-powered Anson single-seater. Gillian is another fast lady who has excelled on horseback and is also a competitive circuit racer: in July 1985 she dipped into the 28s with a 28.88sec record, at the same time setting BTD.

Joy Rainey has held the ladies' record at Shelsley for longer than anyone else – in all for an almost uninterrupted 23 years.

Nothing daunted, Joy got herself into a potent single-seater too. She procured a 2.3-litre Hart-powered Pilbeam which was modified to her requirements, and set herself the goal of retaking the record from Gillian. The result in August 1986 was an almost superhuman 28.32sec. It was to stand as the ladies' record for 16 years.

Gillian, now Mrs Goldsmith, continued to be active at Shelsley thanks to the patronage of Terry Grainger, who offered drives in his Lotus 23B and

ex-Oscar Moore HWM-Jaguar to several women racers, including Penny Griffiths, Georgina Baillie Hill, former downhill skier Divina Galica, Amanda Stretton and Lisa Strangward. Gillian has proved to be consistently the fastest of Terry's protégés, and got her times in the now methanol-fuelled Lotus, running in the pre-1972 classic class, down to 31.67. Georgina Baillie Hill also competed very effectively in her own Emeryson-Climax and Elva-BMW sports-racers.

Shelsley has continued to attract women drivers, consistently among them Lynn Owen, Lynne Whitehead and Sandra Tomlin. It was Sandra who finally broke Joy Rainey's long-standing record in September 2002, shaving 0.11sec off it with her 2.8-litre Pilbeam MP58H. The daughter of Phil Chapman, who built and campaigned a succession of fierce Chapman-Mercury sports-racing Specials, and the mother of Oliver and Amy, Sandra is part of a three-generation hillclimbing family. Then in 2004 Sue Young started to get to grips with her husband Deryk's mighty 4-litre Dellara-Judd. In June she set a new record in 27.77sec, and six weeks later became the first woman to beat 27 seconds with a storming 26.98sec climb. Dorothy Levitt, May Cunliffe, Kay Petre and Patsy Burt would all be proud of her.

Sue Young blasts off the line in August 2004 to become the first lady to climb Shelsley Walsh in under 27 seconds.

THE 26-SEC DECADE
1980–1989

As the 1980s began, the stars at the end of the previous decade – Douglas-Osborn, Griffiths, Lane, Franklin, Cramer – continued to hold sway. The 1980 season was of course Shelsley's 75th anniversary and it was a vintage year. In June Roy Lane's latest March-DFV took 0.12sec off Alister Douglas-Osborn's record, only for ADO to pulverise that minutes later with the first sub-27 time, a thrilling 26.71 in the Pilbeam-DFV. In July, with ADO absent, there was a rare dead-heat for BTD between Martyn Griffiths, now with 2.5-litres of Hart in his Pilbeam, and Lane. Both clocked 26.99s on their first run. The second run decided

OPPOSITE: After winning the title in 1979, Martyn Griffiths took the record in August 1980 with his four-cylinder Pilbeam-Hart.

BELOW: Clutching his BTD trophy, new record holder Griffiths makes an acceptance speech. MAC president Tony Griffiths is on the right.

it, for Lane was slower while Griffiths, remarkably, did exactly 26.99 again. Then in August, with ADO using a borrowed car – he'd destroyed the MP31 in a big accident at Fintray – Griffiths really wound himself up to climb in 26.60sec. It was his first Shelsley record, and the first time a four-cylinder car had taken the record for 16 years. Lane was second and Cramer, racking up points towards his first championship title, was third.

That August meeting was the one officially celebrating the anniversary, and appropriately an avalanche of new records was achieved in the categories for sports cars (Richard Jones' U2 again, 28.05), GTs (Roland Jones' new Porsche RSR, 32.4sec), special saloons (Barrogill Angus' Stiletto, 31.52sec) and 1600cc single-seaters (Martin Bolsover's March, 28.93sec). Joy Rainey (29.75sec) got the Ladies' Record back from Maggie Blankstone after just five weeks without it, and David Gould took the Shelsley Specials record in 29 dead with his beautiful home-built 1600cc Special. He would of course go on to become one

of the most important racing car constructors for hillclimbers. And, because the Midland Automobile Club is good at anniversaries, there was a heart-warming handicap for cars that had set BTD in times past. On this occasion the immortal Raymond Mays Vauxhall Villiers, driven by Anthony Brooke, vanquished the Basil Davenport Spider, in the hands of Ron Sant.

In 1981 a new challenger to ADO appeared in the shape of James Thomson. Guyson boss Jim Thomson, himself an enthusiastic hillclimber and the sponsor of the RAC Hillclimb Championship, had bought a full-house Pilbeam-Hart for his 20-year-old son. Sensationally, in his first hillclimb season James – a calm, self-contained lad whose only previous experience had been in saloons – won the championship. It was a steep learning curve, however. At the June Shelsley, James showed his inexperience when he went off at the first Ess on his first run and the second Ess on his second. But he came back to the July non-championship meeting and won it, getting within

James Thomson on the line in the Guyson Pilbeam-Hart MP40. He spent just one full season in championship hillclimbing, and won the title.

LEFT: Rare beast at
the May 1981 meeting
was Peter Cook's
3.5-litre Ginetta G16.

BELOW: Formula 1 cars
are always a magical
sight at Shelsley. John
McCartney's 1972 BRM
V12 set BTD at a non-
championship meeting
in 1983.

0.28sec of Griffiths' record, and by September, with a string of BTDs behind him, he'd gained hugely in polish and confidence. On his second championship runs he took 0.12sec off the record, leaving ADO, the final runner, with the pressure he needed to pull something out of the bag. Which is just what the relentless Alister did, with a 26.42sec. Nevertheless, at the end of a long, hard season, young James beat ADO to the title and then, after one magic season in championship

David Lee's elegant Aston Martin-powered Tojeiro climbed in 38.35sec, June 1983.

hillclimbing, he moved on to circuit racing.

There was another new champion in 1982, Martin Bolsover, who re-engined his 1600 March with a 2.5 Hart. At Shelsley, however, ADO continued to be in a class of his own, winning both the big meetings and lowering his record in August by another 0.05sec. Martyn Griffiths, now sharing a new Pilbeam-Hart MP53 with print tycoon Max Harvey, was second in June, and won the July non-Championship event. But in August

his transmission broke, allowing the Pilbeam-Hart of Dave Harris to take a distant second from Cramer and Bolsover.

In 1983 spectator communication was further improved with the adoption of big digital read-out displays showing split times and speeds at the Esses and at the start line. BTD in the June event was set in the class runs by Bolsover, now running as part of the Guyson team. Then another competitor dropped a lot of oil, so the championship climbs were slower – but ADO still came out on top, from Bolsover and Griffiths. In July Griffiths took a rather lonely win on the Saturday, and on the Sunday John McCartney's magnificent 1972 V12 F1 BRM was fastest. In August it was ADO-Bolsover-Griffiths again, with Alister bringing his record down to 26.08 on one of his class runs. But after a tremendously consistent season on the other hills, Bolsover was again champion, Griffiths again runner-up.

For 1984 ADO had a new car, shared with sponsor John Hunt: the latest Pilbeam MP55 with 4.2-litre Cosworth DFY. Martyn Griffiths and Max Harvey upgraded to a new MP53 for last year's 2.8-litre Hart engine. Bolsover, no longer chasing the title above all else, had swapped cars with Jim Thomson's younger son Tim, which put him in a sports-racing Pilbeam MP43. In June, on a hill still slippery after morning rain, ADO won from Tim Thomson and Martyn Griffiths. In August John

Cosworth engineers Paul Squires and Phil Kidsley extracted tremendous power, and noise, from this Brabham BT28, using a supercharged 785cc BDA. This is Phil in 1983.

163

ABOVE: Alister Douglas-Osborn's big DFY-powered Pilbeam had a shortened 1984 season: it was crashed heavily by sharing driver John Hunt at Crossing.

RIGHT: The dominant chassis designer in hillclimbing from the mid-1970s was Mike Pilbeam. Here he seems to be contemplating John Hunt's nasty accident with the MP55.

Hunt crashed the Pilbeam-DFY heavily at Crossing, suffering leg injuries. ADO was left with BTD from his class runs, but had to watch as the championship runs went to Bolsover by 0.04sec from Roy Lane, now using BMW power in his Pilbeam, and Griffiths. While ADO had to rely for the rest of the season on a substitute four-cylinder Pilbeam, Bolsover switched back to his old single-seater for the last three rounds, and took his third title on the trot. He was the first man to do that since Tony Marsh 17 years before.

As always, the championship run-offs soaked up most of the attention, but the battles down the classes were often every bit as close. At the June meeting Porsche protagonists Tony Bancroft and the Garland brothers, Nigel and Peter, finished up with all three covered by 0.06sec, Nigel taking the class from Tony and Peter.

There was an interesting development for 1985

ABOVE: Tony Bancroft, formerly known as Spotty Smith, with his Porsche Turbo at the Top Ess.

LEFT: Roy Lane relied on BMW power in the early 1980s. This is his Pilbeam MP51 at Crossing in 1984.

when Shelsley Specials record holder David Gould further developed his superbly crafted car, replacing its 1600cc engine with a 2.5-litre Hart, and enlisting Chris Cramer as driver. After John Hunt's accident, ADO had now joined the ranks of Pilbeam-Hart pedallers. But it was Roy Lane, now in his 19th year of championship hillclimbing, who came back into the winner's circle in June with the BMW-powered Pilbeam. On a slippery hill he beat Cramer in the Gould by 0.1sec and demoted ADO and Griffiths to third and fourth. At one of the two July one-day meetings another bit of history was made. Griffiths won the Saturday event, but Sunday's BTD went to Gillian Fortescue-Thomas in Alan Payne's tricky V8 Buick-

powered Anson. It was the first, and remains so far the only, time a woman has set BTD at Shelsley, and it also resulted in a new ladies' record.

At the August meeting there was another anniversary to celebrate: 80 years since the first meeting. Once again there was a handicap for cars with great Shelsley history, won by Ron Footitt's Frazer Nash from the ex-Phil Scragg HWM-Jaguar of Clive Richards. The demonstration runs included Uwe Hucke in the four-wheel-drive Bugatti which young Jean Bugatti crashed in practice in 1932. And Tony Marsh was back at the wheel of the 4wd Marsh Special – nearly 20 years after selling the car he was immediately matching his 1967 times.

Martin Bolsover started his third title year in a sports-racing car, the Pilbeam MP43.

Autosport chose this day to present their inaugural John Bolster Trophy to David Gould. Bolster had been the magazine's technical editor from its launch in 1950 until his death in 1984, and the trophy was instituted to acknowledge the sort of technical ingenuity and persistence that characterised his own cars. Given Bolster's love of Shelsley Walsh, and the fact that the Gould-Hart, in Chris Cramer's hands, was leading the Hillclimb Championship at that point, it was a happy choice. John's widow Rosemary presented the trophy, a tantalus with two decanters, one filled with vodka and the other with tomato juice, the ingredients of a Bloody Mary. *Bloody Mary* herself was present as well, on day release from Beaulieu.

The Gould very nearly won the event, in damp slippery conditions, but in the end Martyn Griffiths beat Chris Cramer by a healthy 0.39sec, with Roy Lane third; ADO was absent with 'flu. But Cramer went on to win the championship, and start a line of success for the Gould marque which continues to this day.

ABOVE: *A big car for the narrow hill was Bill Cole's much-modified V12 E-type.*

LEFT: *Champions both: James Thomson (1981) and Martin Bolsover (1982-3-4).*

BED AND BOARD AT SHELSLEY

There is no longer an officially nominated Shelsley hotel, but from the hillclimb's earliest days the officials needed a base from which to prepare for the event. At first this was a pub in the village of Stanford Bridge, rather grandly called the Stanford Bridge Hotel. Leslie Wilson's son Roger, who from a schoolboy used to help his father with the organisation, remembered it well:

Like countless other country inns long divested of its carriage trade, it had not yet fully adapted to the motoring era, although there was a petrol pump next door. We dined on succulent roast lamb in a tiny back parlour, just as a traveller in a post-chaise might have done a century before, and carried candles up to bed.

Leslie Wilson, who was obviously fond of the place, was perturbed to find that one of the trusty staff had changed jobs, and asked for him to be transferred back again. The MAC files contain a brisk note in his neat handwriting, which says:

The valet we have been accustomed to having is now the hall porter at the Midland Conservative Club. Arrangements should be made immediately for his services at the hotel for the hillclimb weekend, if possible.

By 1930 the headquarters had moved to the more up-to-date surroundings of the Swan Hotel at Tenbury Wells. This has long since closed its doors: the building still stands, but has now been redeveloped as private housing. In its heyday, however, over a hillclimb weekend every single room would be taken by Shelsley people, officials, drivers, friends and hangers-on. When practice was wet the entire hotel staff would be set to drying out sodden overalls and shoes, and washing and ironing fresh clothes for the next morning. Dinner would be taken by the entire Shelsley party at a long table, and all the talk would be about the event. On an evening after the record had fallen, it would be particularly joyous and noisy. A menu that survives shows that the Swan served plentiful, wholesome

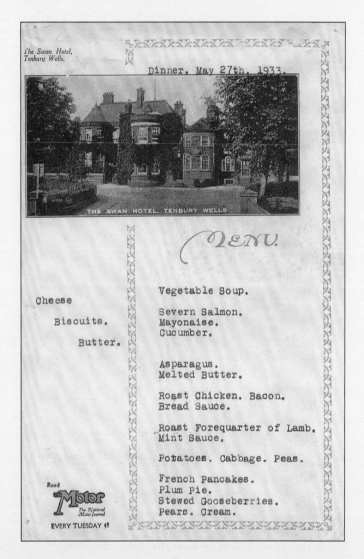

The Swan Hotel,
Tenbury Wells.

Dinner. May 27th. 1933.

THE SWAN HOTEL. TENBURY WELLS

MENU.

Cheese

Biscuits.

Butter.

Vegetable Soup.

Severn Salmon.
Mayonaise.
Cucumber.

Asparagus.
Melted Butter.

Roast Chicken. Bacon.
Bread Sauce.

Roast Forequarter of Lamb.
Mint Sauce.

Potatoes. Cabbage. Peas.

French Pancakes.
Plum Pie.
Stewed Gooseberries.
Pears. Cream.

Read
the Motor
The National
Motor Journal
EVERY TUESDAY 4ᵈ

Dinner at The Swan after Raymond Mays' May 1933 victory with the Villiers Supercharge is a reminder of British fare between the wars.

English food, for those were the days when gravy was acceptable but an elaborate sauce was not, and anything remotely exotic would be condemned by the clientele as "foreign muck".

Nevertheless foreign visitors, carefully wooed by the determined Leslie Wilson, were a great asset for Shelsley:

A good deal of midnight oil was burned waiting up for those who came by road after crossing the Channel to Dover or Folkestone and not

The Bridge at Stanford Bridge.

The Hundred House, Great Witley.

infrequently lost their way. Shelsley Walsh is a mouthful even to most Englishmen. We often feared that Tenbury-bound Frenchmen and Germans might find their way across Wales to Tenby.

It was a great coup when Wilson persuaded Hans Stuck and Rudi Caracciola to make the trip from Germany to compete in the July 1930 Shelsley. But after everything had been arranged and agreed, Wilson received an urgent telegram from Germany saying that they could not come without their dogs – this, of course, was before the days of rabies regulations. Caracciola's wife Charly in particular was devoted to her long-haired honey-coloured dachshund, and the long-suffering Wilson had to make special arrangements with the Swan to ensure that the dogs were adequately catered for. But it was worth the effort, with a new hill record for Stuck and a new sports car mark for Caracciola, and the important visitors were happy. Wilson wrote:

Stuck was very delighted with his success, and I shall never forget the ride with him [in his Austro-Daimler road car] back along the twisty roads to Tenbury as long as I live. Nor the way he put away 12lbs of raspberries and cream at

one sitting at the celebration dinner after the climb.

Raymond Mays chose to avoid the Swan, and stayed as far away as Malvern, always in the Abbey Hotel, which he used from his first visit to the hill in 1921. Mays always had an eye for a deal, and never missed an opportunity to give the Abbey a "plug" in his various writings, so no doubt he

(continued overleaf)

The Talbot at Knightwick.

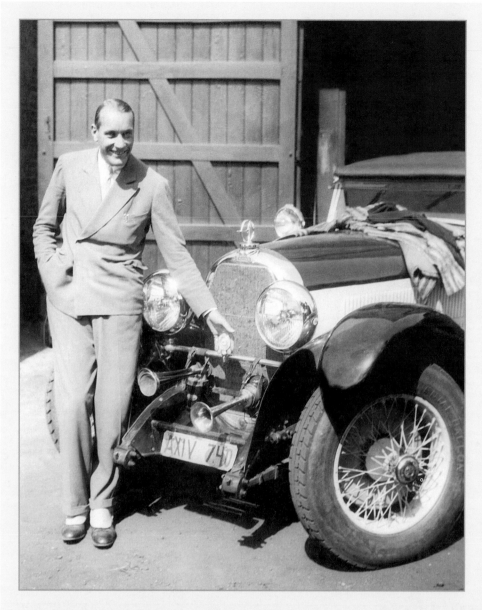

Hans Stuck, in double-breasted suit and spats, poses with his Austro-Daimler road car outside The Swan's garage on the Sunday morning after his 1930 victory.

August weekend: larger-than-life landlord John Moore was a Shelsley competitor with his Morgan. But by the 1960s The Bridge at Stanford Bridge was very much back on the scene. More and more hillclimbers wanted to camp overnight, and Shelsley did not allow camping at the hill. There was a campsite next door to The Bridge, and so the pub became the base for many hillclimb regulars.

In due course the Shelsley landlords relented sufficiently to allow caravans to tether in the lower field, and later tents were permitted too. In modern times many of the serious hillclimbers have invested in luxurious motorhomes, and by the Friday night of a hillclimb weekend there will be several at anchor in the field opposite the paddock. Others on a tighter budget resort to humble tents, and a party atmosphere ensues. Those preferring more conventional comforts usually book into nearby country hotels like the Hundred House in Great Witley or the Manor Arms in Abberley, or one of the several pubs and B&Bs in the area.

(continued from previous page)

negotiated an excellent discount. However the Abbey was used by RAF units during World War II and perhaps wasn't able to accommodate him for the 1946 meeting, so he switched allegiance to the even more distant Lygon Arms at Broadway.

After the war the Swan had gone rather downhill – "lorry drivers and fruit machines" said one regular with a shudder – and MAC officials transferred their patronage to The Elms at Abberley, although this later moved upmarket and became rather expensive. The Noak at Martley actually had its own Noak Shelsley Club for hillclimb supporters for a while, and The Birche at Shelsley Beauchamp used to hold a hillclimbers' party on the Saturday evening of the

Most Shelsley regulars have their own favourites. Nothing would persuade me to stay anywhere else except the wonderful Talbot Inn at Knightwick, where much of the food is home grown, and the fish is freshly caught from the Teme that runs almost past the front door. All the best pubs and B&Bs in the area get fully booked up almost as soon as the new season's dates are announced, for staying in a good Worcestershire hostelry can add enormously to the pleasure of a hillclimbing weekend, and enhance the feeling of taking part in a very English activity.

Star of the 1985 hillclimb season was David Gould's self-built Hart-powered car. With Chris Cramer at the wheel it took the championship – and the John Bolster Trophy.

Dudley Mason-Styrron at the Esses in June 1987 in the magnificent ex-works Tasman single-seater Ferrari he shared with his wife Sally.

ABOVE: Hannu Mikkola
was sensational at the
July 1986 meeting, taking
the works Audi up in an
almost unbelievable
29.51sec.

RIGHT: Mikkola
thoroughly enjoyed his
first visit to Shelsley,
which he treated like a
tarmac rally stage.

ADO was back on top at his favourite hill for the June 1986 meeting, and his 26.27 was the nearest he'd got with the four-cylinder Pilbeam to his eight-cylinder record. Ray Rowan (Pilbeam) took second from Cramer and Griffiths. Then came the two July one-day meetings which, as non-championship rounds, normally attracted less attention.

However there was another anniversary to celebrate – fifty years since Hans Stuck's exciting visit with the Auto Union. The ever-resourceful MAC persuaded Volkswagen-Audi, the current owners of the Auto Union brand, to send former

World Rally Champion Hannu Mikkola to the July weekend with a full-house works Audi Quattro Group B rally car. Neil Corner also brought his superb 1939 D-type Auto Union and did three demonstration climbs.

Mikkola, who had never seen Shelsley Walsh before, attacked the hill as he would a tarmac rally stage, rocketing away from the line with a shriek from all four tyres and hurling the car broadside into the Esses. He got down to a breathtaking 29.51sec – which was BTD for the Saturday meeting. Although this was the fastest ever climb by a closed car, it could not count as a saloon

Neil Corner conjured up echoes of Hans Stuck when he demonstrated his magnificent 1939 V12 Auto Union on the hill in July 1986.

record because the FIA treated Group B cars as sports cars. Nothing daunted, the amazing Nic Mann took his V8 Morris Minor up on the Sunday in 30.49, and that was a new saloon record. The incredible road-going Minor, progressively developed by Nic to find more and more speed and grip, had beaten the previous mark set by Brian Walker in his sophisticated Chevron-based, Hart-powered Skoda silhouette car.

Almost unnoticed in all this excitement, ADO took yet another BTD on the Sunday. It was his 18th at Shelsley, an extraordinary run of success, and it was to be his last. Griffiths won in August, taking BTD in the dry class runs and getting maximum points in the treacherously wet championship runs, ahead of Cramer, Lane and David Gould. That season Griffiths won his second title.

Although 1987 brought Martyn his third, Roy Lane seemed to have inherited the Douglas-Osborn crown as king of Shelsley, for he won both championship rounds. He had a new car which looked ideally suited to the hill, the latest Pilbeam MP58 with 4-litre Cosworth DFL power unit. But at the June meeting Martyn Griffiths and Max Harvey, who was leading the championship at that point, withdrew when a telephone call to Max imparted the horrifying news that a serious fire at one of his print factories had cost the lives of several of his employees. On a slightly damp hill, Lane's BTD of 26.93 was almost a second shy of the record, with Tim Thomson's Pilbeam-Hart second and the powerful 5-litre Pilbeam-Repco of Charles Wardle third. Wardle shared his car with Chris Dowson, son of George Dowson who had campaigned the Lightweight Special with Alec Issigonis 40 years before. Yet again the hillclimb gene was being passed from generation to generation.

Griffiths did get BTD at the July non-championship meeting, with a 26.72, but in August he was beaten fair and square by Lane, whose storming 26.14sec was only 0.06sec off ADO's old record. Roy's speeds through the traps were 120mph at the Esses and 132mph at the finish. Griffiths and Harvey were second and third in their immaculate yellow Pilbeam, prepared at Martin Middleton's garage on Gorcott Hill, where the Midland AC held its first-ever hillclimb back in 1901. Electric tyre warmers had recently become standard wear in Formula 1, and Griffiths and Harvey were the first to use them in hillclimbing,

Nic Mann's extraordinary turbo V8 Morris Minor took the saloon record in 1986 in 30.49sec.

The description "Shelsley stalwart" certainly applies to Bob Dayson, who has long been a fixture in highly-developed Lotus 7 derivatives. This is Bob in August 1986.

where they could offer a real advantage, on the lower parts of the hill at least. Soon all the front-runners were buying them, until it became clear that this expense was either going to be necessary for everybody or else should be outlawed. So they were banned.

Another rule change that had come in for the 1987 season was the insistence by the national governing body that all cars used in competition should have a basic modicum of silencing. Large-diameter stainless steel pots appeared on every exit pipe, and noise was generally reduced to bearable levels without great loss of power. Long-time Shelsley spectators also noted that the hill had become a less aurally atmospheric place with the gradual removal of trees down from the Esses.

Typical of the silhouette saloon philosophy was Brian Walker's Skoda, which under its thin shell was a Chevron-Hart.

Charles Wardle gradually sorted out the 5-litre Pilbeam-Repco until in 1988 he won the June Shelsley, and the Championship.

Ray Rowan's Roman setting BTD at the June 1989 meeting. He went on to win the title that year.

One of the faithful who has rarely missed a meeting in the past 55 years particularly cherishes the memory of unsilenced Bugattis and ERAs echoing up the hill long before they burst into view out of the trees.

The following year brought a new name both to the Shelsley BTD lists and to the roster of National Champions. Charles Wardle had the big Pilbeam-Repco properly sorted out now, and won the June meeting despite spinning on his final run. It was close, though. His 26.81 was just 0.04sec faster than Griffiths and 0.15sec faster than Lane. The Griffiths/Harvey duo had got engine builder Brian Hart to hang a Holset turbocharger on their 2.8-litre Pilbeam four, and at the wet July Shelsley Martyn and Max finished 1-2 ahead of Wardle and Lane, although a future record-holder, Richard Brown, won the Saturday event in his V8 Rover-powered Martin. But Griffiths had a bad day at the August Shelsley. After missing a gear on his first championship run, he was slowed by a shower on his second. Wardle won with 26.24sec from Lane and Chris Dowson.

Ray Rowan had been getting quicker and quicker in his Toleman-based Roman, now shared with Rob Turnbull who supplied its 2.8 Hart engine. Griffiths was unable to do a full season in 1989, but Roy Lane remained faithful to the cause. In June Rowan set the sole Shelsley BTD of his career with a 26.77, which was 0.06sec quicker than Lane. But Lane won in July and August, and his August victory was particularly praiseworthy, because the week before he'd crashed the big silver Pilbeam at the Irish Craigantlet venue, hitting the timekeepers' caravan. After several all-nighters the car looked as immaculate as ever, and in a classic Shelsley cliff-hanger Roy found enough on his final run to beat Rowan by 0.03sec, with Wardle third. But at season's end, the title went to Ray rather than Roy, with just three points in it.

At that August meeting ERA R4D's latest custodian, Anthony Mayman, shattered the pre-war class record with a scintillating 34.61sec climb. But, ironically, there was no pre-war class that day and he was running with post-war cars, so the time couldn't formally count as a new pre-war record. Afterwards Mayman confided to Mark Joseland that he thought R4D was capable of a climb in the 33s. It wasn't until some 15 years later, long after Mayman's tragic suicide, that Mac Hulbert proved him right.

MODERN TIMES 1990–2004

During the last decade of the 20th century, motorsport at every level was booming. There were more and more events, more and more venues, and more and more competition licences being issued to more and more people keen to try their hand. Shelsley was able to share in this growth.

The three weekends' use permitted by the landlords had long since settled into a pattern of two major two-day meetings in June and August, and two one-day meetings in July which were more club-oriented. But in 1992 permission was gained to run a fourth weekend, in September, and for 1998 the Midland AC were able to add a fifth weekend, in May. Two of those five weekends, in May and July, comprise separate one-day meetings on Saturday and Sunday, with practice in the morning. One day of the July weekend is now dedicated to vintage and historic cars, in a wonderfully atmospheric meeting co-promoted with the Vintage Sports-Car Club. The other three weekends follow the traditional format of practice on Saturday, event on Sunday, with the two rounds of the British Hillclimb Championship happening in June and August.

With so many events, and up to 220 competitors in each, it would need a far bigger book than this to focus on all the excellent battles throughout all the classes, with the record in each category invariably fought over as keenly as the outright record for the hill. Indeed, getting an entry for the major meetings can be a problem, for they are always over-subscribed – which

Graeme Wight Junior's tremendous commitment made him unbeatable in 2002 and 2003 in the V6 Gould, and in June 2003 he broke 25 seconds for the first time – and by a healthy margin.

Typical busy Shelsley paddock scene as cars and drivers queue up in the sunshine for their practice runs.

ABOVE: August 1990: Martyn Griffiths launches the Pilbeam MP58 on his final run, intent on breaking "that bloody record". He did just that, taking the record below 26 seconds for the first time.

OPPOSITE LEFT: Former World Champion John Surtees enjoys a ride up Shelsley astride a Manx Norton in 1991 . . . and (LEFT) shows off his Vincent in the paddock to fellow bike lover Denis Jenkinson.

Richard Brown said the MP58 was so easy to drive a monkey could do it, but his 25.34 in 1992 stood unbeaten for nine years.

ensures that the non-championship meetings are just as high in quality. But as ever it was the Top Twelve run-offs for championship points which continued to get the lion's share of the glory, and the media attention.

Martyn Griffiths and Max Harvey came back with a bang in 1990. They bought one of Mike Pilbeam's superb new MP58 chassis, and installed the latest Cosworth DFR F1 engine. Griffiths won in June with a 26.16sec, 0.24sec clear of Roy Lane's Pilbeam-DFL, with David Gould's increasingly rapid son Sean third in the now venerable Gould-Hart, and Harvey fourth. But still Alister Douglas-Osborn's long-standing record of 26.08 was unbeaten, after seven years. Martyn had two

ambitions: "to break that bloody record, and climb Shelsley in a twenty-five-point-something". Finally in August he did both. It was Martyn's favourite scenario. Running last, he had already won the meeting and 10 championship points with his first run, so on that final run he had nothing to lose. Through Kennel, Crossing, Bottom and Top Ess, it was a perfect, charging effort, crossing the finish line at 135mph. The clocks were stopped at 25.86. It was the high spot of a great year for Griffiths, which netted his fourth championship, ahead of Lane, Rowan and partner Harvey. This meeting brought another anniversary for the MAC to celebrate – the 90th since the formation of the club. Among the special guests was John Surtees,

who took a 1000cc Vincent up the hill in an enthralling 36.52sec.

Martyn Griffiths' fifth title came in 1991, along with Shelsley BTDs in June – by just 0.18sec from the evergreen Roy Lane, as Ray Rowan crashed heavily after the Crossing – and August, when the margin to Lane was even less at 0.05sec. Charles Wardle had the old Pilbeam-Repco going well again for third, ahead of Max Harvey. Over the July weekend Lane beat Wardle by 0.11sec for BTD on the Sunday, while on the vintage Saturday, Anthony Mayman formally took his pre-war record under 35 seconds with the famous ex-Mays, ex-Wharton ERA R4D, this time climbing in 34.97sec.

That August win was Griffiths' 18th Shelsley BTD,

and his last. After five championship titles – more than anyone else save Tony Marsh – he decided it was time to stop. The yellow Pilbeam-DFR was sold to David Grace and Richard Brown, and Martyn and Max Harvey went classic rallying instead.

That winter the hill was completely resurfaced, at a cost to the MAC of £30,000, and at the June 1992 meeting Richard Brown, who was not making a concerted attack on the championship, emerged as a hillclimber of brilliance. He took 0.01sec off the hill record on his first class run, and then on his first championship run he brought the record down to a remarkable 25.34sec. Modestly he put this down to the car: "It's such a phenomenal thing to drive, a monkey could do it". That record

Tom Hammonds beat even Hannu Mikkola's Audi time with his ferocious Pike's Peak replica. His 28.58 closed car record from 1992 still stood in 2005.

ABOVE: David Grace's August 1993 victory with the now black and silver MP58 helped him to his first championship title.

RIGHT: David Grace's five titles put him on a par with Martyn Griffiths and just one behind Tony Marsh.

was to stand for nine years. Grace might have gone even faster in the same car had he not missed a gear coming out of the Esses. He ended up second, with Lane third.

Several class records were also broken on the new surface, notably by Audi specialist Tom Hammonds, whose full-house Pike's Peak replica quattro pulverised Hannu Mikkola's 1986 time with a remarkable 28.58sec, an unbelievable speed for a closed car. Another superb effort came from Tim Barrington, whose Vision took a clear second, all but a hundredth, off the 1600cc racing car class record to leave it at 27.46sec. In July Lane had an easy win in the absence of the other fast boys, but in the August championship round the Pilbeam-DFR finished first and second, with Grace besting Brown by 0.15sec: but he was still 0.22 off Brown's record. Grace won the new September Midland championship date as well, but against less opposition. As for the final standings, at the end of the year David Grace and Roy Lane were tied on points, with the title going to Roy on the basis of the extra dropped scores.

The June 1993 meeting brought another new name to the BTD roster: Mark Colton, in the Ray Rowan-built Roman, now with 3.5-litre Judd power. He dipped into the 25s with a 25.96, besting both David Grace and Roy Lane in a furious run which produced a finish line speed of 144mph. Roy took his customary July victory, but the August meeting was tense indeed, for the reigning champion and runner-up arrived one point apart in the championship. Grace won it with a 25.57, with Lane third behind Colton, and

Grace went on to win his first national title by a single point from Lane. In September Graham Hickman – who finished fourth in the championship with his Pilbeam-DFR behind third man Colton – set BTD amid less exalted company.

Colton repeated his June success in 1994, still more than half a second off the record. David Grace missed the championship runs after his co-driver, Noel le Tissier, crashed at Kennel. The traditional iron fencing on the left of the track sliced into the Pilbeam's monocoque, passing between the driver's legs, and it was only after this incident that the Midland AC persuaded the Shelsley landlord that the fencing should be

Richard Drewett's big V8 Lotuses down the years have included Types 15, 29, 30 and 70. This is the 30 which set BTD in July 1994.

Andy Priaulx was just 22 when he clinched the 1995 championship with BTD at the August Shelsley.

removed. Roy Lane, with a new Judd EV F1 engine and a new Pilbeam chassis, was second. Third was a less familiar name: 20-year-old Andy Priaulx from Guernsey, whose father Graham had been hillclimbing for years and had invested the previous year in the ex-David Grace Pilbeam-Hart. Andy had learned fast, and was definitely a man to watch. In August it was Colton again in the green and orange Roman, with Lane second once more and Grace third. But the season ended with a second title for Grace, by just two points from Colton.

The July non-championship weekend was full of action. On Saturday Richard Drewett's big Lotus 30 sports-racer took BTD in 32.77sec, with Duncan Ricketts' ERA R1B setting a pre-war 1500cc class record with 34.88sec. Then on Sunday

Graham Hickman hit the bank at Crossing when the rear suspension of his ex-F1 Jordan-DFR broke. The Jordan cartwheeled off to the left, ending up in the undergrowth 30 feet from the track, upside down. Hickman was taken to hospital with a fractured skull and injured shoulder, but he had the small consolation that his earlier run was BTD. At the September meeting, on a wet and greasy hill, Roy Lane added yet another BTD to his Shelsley tally.

It was in 1995 that Andy Priaulx came into his own, for father Graham had now purchased a 4.0 Pilbeam-DFL. He set a 26.59 BTD at the June Shelsley in the class runs, but in the run-off Graham had just made his run when the heavens opened and drenched the hill. That left Graham with 10 points ahead of Roger Moran's 2-litre

Pilbeam and Peter Harper's Vision-Hart. Before the rain, Peter Garland set a production sports car record with a 31.93sec in his road-going Morgan Plus 8. Roy Lane took BTD at the new two-day event at the start of July, once again racking up points in the Midland Hillclimb Championship which he had almost made his own over the years: the Pilbeam-Judds of Patrick Wood and Tim Mason were second and third. At the Saturday VSCC meeting in July Guy Smith's Alvis-engined Frazer-Nash single-seater was fastest, with John Beattie taking the Sunday honours in his SPA-Judd.

In August the hillclimbing world was devastated by the death of one of its top drivers. Championship runner-up Mark Colton was killed in a 130mph accident in the Northern Ireland round at Craigantlet. The following week the championship circus was in sombre mood at Shelsley, and everyone stood for a minute's silence in Mark's memory. Then Andy Priaulx went out and set BTD in 26.12sec, enough to confirm him as RAC Hillclimb Champion at just 22 years of age. By the end of the year Priaulx had scored 10 victories, and as the points system allowed each driver to count only his best 10 scores, he had a maximum 100 points – the most dominating performance since Roy Lane's string of victories 20 years before. By the next season Priaulx had moved on from hillclimbing to begin a successful professional career in circuit racing.

For 1996 Roger Moran joined the big boys with a new Pilbeam-Judd MP72. By contrast, David Grace had sold his Pilbeam but kept the DFR engine, putting this into one of David Gould's new

Guy Smith's exploits with his potent Alvis-powered Frazer Nash single-seater included BTDs at VSCC Shelsleys in 1993 and 1995.

Mark Colton's finest Shelsley moment was this sub-26 BTD in June 1993 in the Roman-Judd, two years before his tragic death in an Irish hillclimb.

Ralt-based chassis. Gould had bought a stock of redundant RT37 carbonfibre monocoques and other parts from Ron Tauranac's Ralt operation, and built them into very stiff, very effective hillclimb cars which he called Gould-Ralt GR37s. But Roy Lane's faithful Pilbeam-Judd was fastest at the June Shelsley, from Moran and Grace, with Patrick Wood's Pilbeam-DFZ fourth. This event was a round of the FIA International Hillclimb Challenge, just as in the 1930s it briefly supplied a round of the European Hillclimb Championship. Belgian Christian Hauser made the trip with his 2.5 Martini-BMW, but found the course much shorter than the mountain settings he was accustomed to, although his 28.51sec climb was respectable enough.

The July weekend saw another Gould-Ralt, Richard Fry's 2.5 Hart-powered version, set BTD on Sunday, with John Venables-Llewellyn in Rodney Felton's magnificent Alfa P3 taking VSCC honours on the Saturday. For the August Championship round, the hill was slippery after overnight rain – during the class runs, said Jerry Sturman's *Autosport* report, "the ominous thump of glassfibre on earth bank was heard with monotonous regularity". David Grace won, from Lane, Wood and Moran. But at season's end the evergreen Roy Lane, aged 61, who first scored championship points 29 seasons earlier, took his fourth British title. For good measure Roy won the Midland Championship round in September from Wood and Simon Durling's Pilbeam-DFL.

In 1997 the British Hillclimb Championship celebrated its half-century – an eventful 50 years since, over a mere five rounds, Raymond Mays vanquished George Abecassis and Dennis Poore to take the inaugural title. Shelsley Walsh had been a pillar of the championship throughout, with always one round and, since 1958, two rounds in every season, so it was only right that this should be the venue for the anniversary celebration. At the June meeting a wonderful gathering of past champions was arranged, including several who were competing anyway. Tony Marsh was there of course, plus the guesting Chris Cramer and David Franklin, but also David Boshier-Jones, Arthur Owen, David Good, Peter Westbury, Peter Lawson and Alister Douglas-Osborn. David Grace won the

Roy Lane's dedication to hillclimbing over more than 30 years has been unrivalled. In 1996 his silver Pilbeam-Judd carried him to his fourth championship title.

The June 1996 meeting brought Christian Hauser's 2.5 Martini Mk 69 in search of European Hillclimb Championship points.

event in the Gould-Ralt, although times were still generally a second shy of Richard Brown's long-standing record. Roy Lane and Roger Moran completed the top trio, covered by 0.28sec.

In July Richard Fry repeated his win of the year before, with Bruce Spollon in ERA R8C taking the Saturday VSCC honours, and then the Grace/Lane battle was on again in August. This time another little bit of Shelsley history was made, because amazingly the Gould/Ralt and the Pilbeam dead-heated, to the hundredth of a second. Both David and Roy climbed in 26.29sec, so their second run times had to be used to decide the winner, which was Grace. Moran and Durling were third and fourth. But in September Lane won again, with a splendid 26.09 – the fastest climb for three years. As for the championship, the season ended with Roger Moran and David Grace tied on points, but after taking best positions into account the title went to Moran.

David Grace then knuckled down to three years

of intense effort at the championship, which would result in the first unbroken trio of titles for any driver since Martin Bolsover 16 years before. Roger Moran was his closest challenger each year. Moran got some useful practice at the May 1998 non-Championship meeting, taking BTD from Rob Turnbull's Gould GR37-DFR – the Ralt part of the name having been dropped, as the Goulds were very much David Gould's own achievement by now. But the June championship round was conclusively Grace's, his 26.07 well clear of Lane and Moran.

The August round, however, was different. Grace had already clinched the title, but in Saturday practice he had a big accident when the Gould bottomed in the bumpy 120mph kink between Crossing and the Esses, and the rear suspension broke. The badly damaged car was rushed back to David Gould's Newbury base, and Grace's wrench Ian Dayson worked through the night to repair it. Such commitment when the championship had

ABOVE: To celebrate 50 years of the British Hillclimb Championship, 17 champions posed at the June 1997 meeting. Back row (from left): Chris Cramer, Andy Priaulx, Alister Douglas-Osborn, James Thomson, Roy Lane, Arthur Owen, Peter Westbury, Charles Wardle. Front row (from left): Peter Lawson, David Grace, David Boshier-Jones, David Franklin, Ray Rowan, Tony Marsh, David Good, Martyn Griffiths, Martin Bolsover.

LEFT: The 1997 championship anniversary celebrations tempted Alister Douglas-Osborn back into the cockpit of a Pilbeam.

ABOVE: A recreation of the 1968 Healey SR Le Mans car ran at the July 1998 Shelsley in the hands of owner Tom Barr-Smith and Martyn Griffiths, who set fastest classic sports car time in 36.12sec.

RIGHT: In August 2002 one of that year's MG EX257 Le Mans cars was demonstrated by team driver Kevin McGarrity.

already been won was typical of him – and that day's Man of the Meeting Award, rather than going to a driver, was rightly awarded to Dayson. Nevertheless, BTD went to Roy Lane in the class runs, while Moran won the run-off from Grace and Turnbull – after Lane had a suspension failure on exactly the same bump that had prompted Grace's accident. Earlier, at the July weekend, the modern-day victory was taken by Tom Hammonds in the Audi, while Julian Mazjub's lovely Bugatti Type 35B won the VSCC Saturday event.

For 1999 Roger Thomas succeeded Mark Joseland as club secretary, and at the same time

the British Hillclimb Championship went through a major change. The MSA, Britain's motorsport governing body, had ceded the task of organising and promoting the championship to Tony Fletcher. Since the 1950s, the championship points had been fought over in two runs at the end of the day: the fastest 10 drivers in the class runs (later fastest 12) would qualify for the run-offs, when each would get two runs to decide the ten top finishers who would earn points from 10 down to 1. This meant that each meeting ended with an exciting climax: but there were some who felt that spectators might weary of waiting through

Roger Moran won the championship in 1997, and spent the next three years chasing David Grace. This is his Pilbeam-Judd at the Top Ess in 1998.

A perfect line through Crossing: Mark Waldron (TVR Tuscan) cuts it close, August 1995.

all the class runs before the championship finale, and perhaps even have gone home. There is rarely much danger of spectators at a football match leaving before the final whistle, but nevertheless a new format was instituted whereby there would be a single Top Twelve run-off in the middle of the afternoon, when all the classes had had their first run, and that would constitute an entire round of the championship. Then there would be another single Top Twelve run-off at the end, again constituting a separate championship round.

The new arrangement had its detractors, who felt that it diminished the championship runs by favouring a conservative approach. In the past, with two runs at his disposal, a competitor could use his first run as a "banker" and then go all-out on his second run. This, for example, was how Martyn Griffiths broke the record in 1990: he knew his first run had been enough to score maximum points and he could risk all on his second. Reigning champion David Grace was philosophical about the changes, although he acknowledged that a significantly different approach was required. "It didn't really make any odds whether I liked it more or less. My job was to take on board whatever challenge the Hillclimb Championship threw at me, and do my best to meet that challenge."

Which is exactly what he did. At the June meeting he hadn't quite got fired up in the first run-off, and finished third behind Moran and Deryk Young's Pilbeam-Judd. But he flew in the second, to beat Moran by a tenth of a second and set BTD.

In August it was once again the turn of the old man to show the youngsters the way. In a brilliant performance, Roy Lane won both rounds – the first by a hundredth of a second from Rob Turnbull, the second by 0.17sec from Grace – to score his 20th Shelsley BTD. In the non-championship events, Tom Hammonds took two more BTDs with the Audi in May and July. Richard Drewett's Lotus 70 won on the July Sunday, and Roger Moran the September weekend. Ironically, despite the new format, the final order in the championship was exactly as it had been the year before: Grace, from Moran and Lane.

Come 2000, going for a fifth title and a third on the trot, Grace was invincible at the June Shelsley, winning both rounds. Roy Lane was second from Roger Moran in the first run-off, and in the second it was the young Scotsman Graeme Wight Junior who vanquished Tim Mason (Gould-Judd) and Lane. Junior had been shaping up as an exciting new challenger for a while, sharing a 1600cc Pilbeam with his father Graeme Senior and

LEFT: *Before going on to serious single-seaters, F1 aerodynamicist Willem Toet cut his hillclimbing teeth with this highly-modified Peugeot 205. In 1993 it set a class record which stood for more than a decade.*

BELOW: *A Shelsley weekend doesn't just involve rushing up the hill on the limit; relaxing in the paddock between runs is all part of the fun. Some of the historic F3 class enjoy a picnic at the June 1991 meeting while, behind, the road-going Ferrari class is lined up.*

The Historic 500cc Racing Car class continues to be popular at Shelsley. Heading the line-up in the paddock feeder road are Paul Harris (BJR-JAP) and David Docherty (Cooper Mk IX).

gradually going further afield from their northerly base. Then they commissioned an intriguing new car from David Gould. Smaller and lighter than the successful Judd- and DFR-engined variants, it used a 2.5-litre V6 Cosworth engine originally intended for an Opel touring car race programme, fed by an air intake incorporated in the roll-over bar and driving through an X-trac six-speed sequential gearbox. Junior spent 2000 getting to know the car, and serving notice that he was going to be extremely quick: his time at the June Shelsley was second BTD.

At the August Shelsley the pundits were forecasting a Grace/Wight shoot-out: but you could never reckon without Roy Lane. Roy got down to an excellent 26.05sec to win the first run-off from Grace and Moran, with Wight fourth. Then it rained. Lane's time remained BTD, and a surprise winner of the second run-off was Willem Toet. For many years a keen hillclimber, Willem was a top Formula 1 aerodynamicist by profession,

working in turn for the Benetton, Ferrari and BAR teams. With his Benetton colleague Richard Marshall, an electronics specialist, he originally campaigned a cleverly modified Peugeot 205 saloon, which went faster and faster as the pair made more and more alterations to it. Toet then moved on to single-seaters, but this day at Shelsley his own Pilbeam failed. So he borrowed a ride in Karl Davison's 4-litre Gould-Judd – and scored his first 10 points ahead of Ben Butterfield, consistently one of the fastest of the 2-litre boys in his Gould Dallara-Vauxhall, which he shared with his enthusiastic mentor Leon Bachelier.

Starring in the July weekend were VSCC man Charles Dean, whose Bugatti Type 51 climbed impressively in under 36 seconds, and Chris Drewett in his 22-year-old 2-litre March, with 30.69sec. Fastest in the September meeting was clubmen's stalwart Brian Moyse with his U2, which achieved 33sec dead.

So David Grace had his fifth title, and moved

on to other things. His DFR Cosworth had proved to be perhaps the most successful hillclimb engine of all time. First in the Griffiths Pilbeam and then in David's Gould, this same V8 unit had in 11 years won the championship seven times and finished second three times. It was also responsible for Richard Brown's historic 25.34sec record, which had stood for almost a decade. There was still no sign of that time being beaten: indeed no-one had dipped into the 25s for more than six years. Some years earlier that wonderful hillclimb enthusiast Reg Phillips, of Fairley Special fame, had offered a £1000 prize out of his own pocket to the first driver to climb Shelsley in under 25 seconds. It seemed that Reg's money was pretty safe.

But for 2001, the Midland AC's centennial year, there had been some resurfacing on the high-speed kink before the Esses – although it remained bumpy. And Graeme Wight Junior had now settled in to the little V6 Gould, and was flinging it up the hills with tremendous courage

and commitment. The talented Scot was digging deep, taking a last drag on a cigarette before getting into the car, and taking fags and lighter up the hill in his overalls pocket so he could have the next one as he switched off at the top and came back down to earth.

It was at the first meeting of the year, in June, that the nine-year hill record finally fell. The margin was small – just six hundredths of a second – but it was a landmark day when the longest-standing outright record in Shelsley's history (except in time of war) was finally breached. In the first run-offs Tim Coventry beat Junior in his 3.5 Gould-Judd, but spun at the Esses in the second bout, handing the runner-up place to Tim Mason's Gould-Judd. David Gould's chassis were now clearly dominating the top branches of the hillclimbing tree.

In the July championship round Junior won both run-offs, but was 0.22sec short of his new record. Goulds filled the top four positions,

Getting down to it: Tim Cameron concentrates hard as he leaves the line in his Cooper 500, August 1989.

ABOVE: Motorcycles now run twice a year at Shelsley, and the bikers add their own special atmosphere. This is their corner of the paddock in August 1999.

RIGHT: The bikes are nothing if not spectacular. Pulling a wheelie off the start is Alan Jolly's 640cc CCM.

Two takes on the sidecar class: Patrick and Paul Keates on their 1052cc Baker F1 (ABOVE) and the transverse-engined, twin-rear-drive FRS of Fred Reeve and Jack Woods.

You don't need an expensive car to go hillclimbing, witness John Newton's smart Mk 1 Austin-Healey Sprite . . .

shared between Coventry, Mason and Rob Turnbull, who were using 3.5-litre DFR power. But several class records fell that day, including 28.87sec for Paul Haimes' 2-litre Mallock, 28.24sec for Mark Budgett's little 1100 Suzuki-powered Force, and a remarkable 27.15sec for Ben Butterfield's 2-litre Dallara-Vauxhall, which was well into the championship points.

After an early August two-day weekend which brought BTDs for Mark Budgett in the Force and Bill Morris (2.0 Pilbeam), there was a huge crowd for the official club centenary celebrations two weeks later. Once more the MAC did a wonderful job of recreating history, and the paddock was full of former champions who had been persuaded to take part.

Tony Marsh was in the 4wd Marsh Special, Roy Lane brought out his McRae-Chevrolet, Mike MacDowel had an outing in the type of Cooper single-seater he used to circuit-race in the 1950s,

Martyn Griffiths was back in a Pilbeam, and Chris Cramer and David Grace were in Goulds. David Franklin was electrifying in the very special Ferrari 212E flat-12, built for Peter Schetty to campaign in European mountain events. Peter Westbury got back into the Felday-Daimler which had been beautifully rebuilt by Ron Welsh, and David Good was spectacular in Donald Day's ERA. But the best ERA time came when David Morris took R11B up in 34.31sec, demolishing Anthony Mayman's outright pre-war record. BTD went to Graeme Wight Junior, of course, but without another new record, and Ken Sims' ferocious Metro 6R4 won the Saturday event.

Basil Davenport's immortal *Spider* appropriately won the Shelsley Specials class in the hands of David Leigh, and Russ Ward, for so long a pillar of hillclimbing at Shelsley and elsewhere, was very rapid in his Chevron B42 single-seater with 4.5-litre V8 Rover power. Other awe-inspiring

. . . and the deceptively rapid Volvo 122S of John Pascoe.

LEFT: This home-brewed monster is the 5.3-litre V12 Jagernaut. A visitor from Guernsey, it is shared by Tara Harvey, seen here in 2003, and Peter Clarke.

ABOVE: Has any car climbed Shelsley as often as Spider? Today it looks just the same, and still travels indecently fast in the hands of David Leigh.

RIGHT: Spider being fettled among more modern machinery in the paddock. Keeping to Davenport tradition, David Leigh wears a brown cow gown when working on the car.

ABOVE: Lukas Huni brought the Type 53 4wd Bugatti to the MAC's 2001 Centenary meeting and, 69 years after Jean Bugatti's embarrassment, it really did get to the top of the hill.

LEFT: Martin Stretton was entrusted with the sensational six-wheel F1 Tyrrell.

Martin Stretton in an earlier single-seater, storming the Esses in Mark Joseland's Frazer Nash Terror III.

visitors to the hill included Mark Walker's 1908 Grand Prix Panhard, Robin Baker's 27-litre Hispano-Delage, and Martin Walford in two of Dean Butler's magnificent Indianapolis cars, the Miller and the straight-eight Maserati. And, following Shelsley's tradition for bringing dramatic Grand Prix cars to Shelsley – Auto Union, V16 BRM and the like – the six-wheel Tyrrell P34 appeared in the hands of Martin Stretton, although it ended in the Esses barriers on the second run.

It was one of the most memorable meetings ever at Shelsley and, for this weekend only, the regulations for the special invitation class discreetly stated that cars had to be silenced "in accordance with regulations in force at time of manufacture". What this meant, of course, was that for these historic guests a blind eye, or rather a blocked ear, was turned to open exhausts. Added to the sights and smells, therefore, were the unadulterated sounds of yesteryear echoing across the Teme Valley to remind us all why Shelsley Walsh is the very stuff of real motorsport.

Graeme Wight Junior went on to be crowned the new British Hillclimb Champion – the first Scot to hold the title.

Roger Moran set the final BTD of the MAC's centennial year in his Gould-Judd at the September meeting. This happened a few days after the dreadful 9/11 terrorist attacks in the USA. Not for the first time, events in the outside world made themselves felt on Shelsley, for the little church was unusually packed with hillclimbers on that Sunday morning.

For 2002 the Shelsley calendar took on the pattern that it still holds: full weekend championship rounds in June and August, a full weekend Midland Championship round in September, and double one-day meetings on weekends in May and July, the latter including a co-promotion with the VSCC. Over the winter, new asphalt had been laid on the start line, and for the June meeting conditions were perfect. This brought a whole slew of new class records, including a Caterham in the 29s (Dave Kimberley, Caterham-Vauxhall, 29.76sec)

ABOVE: The class for clubman's cars, now called Hillclimb Supersports, is always close-fought. Piers Thynne's Mallock charges up to Kennel in August 2003.

LEFT: Club officials like to enjoy the fun as well. This is MAC chairman John Wood in his faithful Ralt.

Friends like to share cars, even at the top level. Simon Durling sits on the back wheel of his Gould while Willem Toet psyches himself up.

and a 2-litre single-seater in the 26s (Trevor Willis, OMS-Vauxhall, 26.45sec). In the first run-offs Graeme Wight Junior attacked with typical aggression, hitting 126mph before the Esses and stopping the clocks at a sensational 24.85sec. It was 0.43sec off his old record – and it was the first ever Shelsley climb in the 24s. Dear old Reg Phillips, at the age of 87, wrote out the £1000 cheque with alacrity. Tim Mason and Rob Turnbull were next up, but in the second run-offs Junior was sidelined with a broken diff, just as Deryk Young hit top form with his Dallara-Judd to take his first-ever 10 points, with Simon Durling just a fifth of a second slower in his 4.0 Gould-DFL. Meanwhile, among the class winners was a young red-haired lad called Adam Fleetwood, who took his little OMS-Kawasaki up in a smoothly impressive 28.37sec. One or two people marked him out as a man to watch.

Junior continued on his winning ways, taking both run-offs at the August meeting on the way

to his second consecutive title with a best of 25.16sec. In the first he was chased by Martin Groves (4.0 Gould-Judd) and Deryk Young, and in the second by Tim Mason, with Groves and Young tying for third. Once again there were plenty of new class records, including an astonishing 27.52sec for Mark Budgett and the little Force.

In the other meetings, Deryk Young ruled both the May and September weekends. Mac Hulbert in Raymond Mays' old ERA R4D took VSCC BTD in July but missed the class record by less than a fifth of a second, and Martin Baker's 1.3 OMS took the other July date. The following May, Deryk Young won again on the Sunday, but Tony Marsh in his 4.0 Gould took Saturday honours – no less than 48 years after his first Shelsley BTD, and 36 years since his last.

For 2003 Roger Fleetwood had ordered a new Gould GR55, with Nicholson-McLaren XB power, to share with his son. Young Adam wasted little time adapting to this bigger car. But Graeme Wight Junior still had the legs of everyone at the June championship round. He lowered his record to 24.78sec in the class runs, then was beaten by Tim Mason in the first run-offs. But in the second run-off the Scot found some more, and left the record at 24.56sec. Adam Fleetwood was flying too, and also got under the old record to set second BTD and pile more pressure on Wight. Shelsley is a horsepower hill, and Graeme was realising that the latest Goulds could match his little V6 car's handling, and make use of their extra grunt.

The Wight/Fleetwood battle reached its zenith in August. Adam was now leading the British Championship, and he confidently took the first run-offs with a 24.72, 0.08sec faster than Graeme, with Martin Groves' more elderly ex-Tony Marsh 3.5 Gould-DFR a strong third. In the second run-offs Wight made one of his ultimate efforts, and got to within 0.03sec of his own record to push Fleetwood down to second, with Groves again third. The championship meeting had been on the Saturday, with an invitation event run on Sunday which was won at a slightly slower speed by Fleetwood – the Wights had set off home for Scotland by then – but at season's end the championship title had gone to Fleetwood. Once more the August Shelsley was a weekend of class records, with Roy Standley's standard-looking Mitsubishi Evo again lowering its own production saloon mark to a remarkable 31.37sec, Mark Budgett finding another fifth of a second, and Martin Stretton borrowing Mark Goodyear's Vision to set a new Supersports record in 28.67sec.

Craig Jones goes for the finish in his Morgan. Combining torque, light weight and simplicity, the Plus 8 makes an excellent hillclimb car.

Two lifetimes in motorsport, and countless climbs up Shelsley Walsh, are represented by those unrelenting enthusiasts, Tony Marsh (left) and Roy Lane.

The September 2003 Shelsley was rather special. Between 1923 and 1950 Raymond Mays set BTD on the hill 21 times, another record that used to seem unbeatable. But the evergreen Roy Lane had different ideas and, in his new Gould-Judd GR55, he flew up the 1000yds in 24.78sec, crossing the finish line at 143mph to set his 22nd Shelsley BTD and better Raymond Mays' total.

Roy's career has been extraordinary, and stands alone in the annals of British Championship hillclimbing. He first scored points in 1967 in a little 1600cc Cooper, and in the 36 seasons that followed, constantly developing his cars and his skills, he never failed to score. He has been in hillclimbing's top six consistently across five decades, from the sixties to the noughties, and he has won an unrivalled 90 British Championship run-offs. A bout of ill health kept him away from the hills in 2004, but three days after leaving hospital he took the Gould to a Curborough sprint

"to keep my hand in". He set BTD, of course. Approaching his 70th birthday, Roy was planning a full season for 2005.

The June 2004 championship meeting was another classic, with both Fleetwood and Wight raising their game yet further. The hill record was beaten four times during the day: first Fleetwood shaved 0.02sec off Wight's mark, then Wight replied by chopping off a fat 0.3sec. Sitting on the line waiting to follow him, Adam heard the cheers for Junior and wound himself up, launching the GR55-XB at the hill to beat Junior by a further 0.06sec, with Martin Groves third. All agonisingly close stuff, and championship hillclimbing at its very best: but in the second run-offs Wight, trying to make up for the 150bhp deficit of the V6 Gould, lost the car on the bumps before the Esses and bounced off the bank. Adam, with the pressure off, was able to find another tenth to leave the record at a startling 24.08sec – with his father second in the same car, and Willem Toet third in his 4.0 Pilbeam-Judd. Other records that day included a new ladies mark for Sue Young, Ian Fidoe's 28.16sec with his sports libre Pilbeam, Phil Cooke's 26.31 out-pacing the 2-litre cars with his 1600 Force-Suzuki, and a pre-1971 historic record for long-time hillclimber Peter Voigt in the Techcraft-Buick.

By mid-year the Wights had dropped out of a full championship programme to concentrate on developing a new bigger-engined chassis for 2005. But Fleetwood, with his second championship title in his pocket, still had his own challenge to face. Having come within 0.09sec in June, he

arrived at the August meeting with the goal of making the first Shelsley climb in the 23-second bracket. As it turned out, he made it look easy, for on his class run, under threatening skies, he got down to a simply sensational 23.87sec. Yet another Shelsley barrier had been breached. In the run-off he was in the 23s again, although 0.05sec slower: it was enough to beat Martin Groves by more than a second, with Willem Toet third. And then the rain came. Adam won the slippery second run-off from Paul Haimes' Dallara-Opel and Toet. And a month later, at the September meeting, Toet took his own first Shelsley BTD in 24.76 sec.

The earth bank at the Esses is always waiting to bite you if you leave your braking the smallest fraction too late. Nigel White was happily uninjured in this incident at the September 2003 meeting, which is more than can be said for his Brabham BT21B.

COLOPHON

Shelsley's hundredth year was a vintage one, in particular because it saw the first sub-24 climb. But of the other BTDs of the year, one that stood out was Mac Hulbert's attack on his own outright pre-war record with the wonderful old black ERA R4D, the very car with which Raymond Mays scored 16 of his Shelsley BTDs, and brought the record down to 37.37sec before the war. Post-war, Ken Wharton used the same car to break 36 seconds for the first time. The brave and determined Hulbert was able to get below 34 seconds with 33.71sec, an almost unbeliev-able time which underlines not only his skill, but also the excellent state of the ERA and the extent to which the hill surface has improved over the past half-century.

It's perhaps a fitting note on which to end this survey of the first century of hillclimbing at Shelsley Walsh, because at Shelsley you are never far away from the history. The modern Goulds and Pilbeams, with more than 650 horsepower, ultra-stiff chassis, incredibly effective brakes, sophisticated suspension and state of the art aerodynamics, can now cover those steep 1000 yards in literally half the time it took Basil Davenport's *Spider* in 1927, and one-third the time it took Ernest Instone's fully-laden Daimler in 1905.

And yet what becomes ever clearer, the more one studies the story of the world's oldest motorsport track, is not how much it has changed, but how much it has stayed the same: not just the hill itself, and its surroundings, but in particular the frame of mind in which the participants approach it. In the rest of

Family affair: Martin Groves prepares his Gould-DFR in the Shelsley paddock assisted by James, Samantha and Charlotte, while wife Mandy sits on a back wheel with Lisa. Twins Lisa and James attended their first Shelsley at 10 days old.

motorsport, and indeed almost all of 21st century life, that is what has changed the most. But Shelsley still provides its same wonderfully anachronistic mix: very determined, courageous competition and huge will to win existing comfortably alongside friendliness, good humour, camaraderie, and good old-fashioned sporting spirit.

Some of the faithful spectators haven't changed, either. A distinguished handful – they know who they are – have been to just about every meeting since the war, and still toil up to their favourite spot at the Esses at each meeting. One of them has indicated to his executors that when he passes on he would like his ashes to be scattered at Shelsley. Another has spent his working life as a schoolmaster, and many years ago he

caught a small boy reading a magazine under his desk in class. Noting that it was the current issue of *Motor Sport*, he told the boy that his punishment was to be taken to the next Shelsley Walsh meeting, as an important extension of his education. It was a detention that has lasted into adulthood, for that same small boy is now climbing Shelsley in the low 27sec bracket.

In the modern world not much is left that shares Shelsley's extraordinary qualities. That's why we must continue to enjoy it, continue to appreciate it, continue to cherish and protect it. This is motorsport as it used to be, motorsport as it should be, and – let us hope – motorsport that succeeding generations will be able to continue to enjoy, just as it has been enjoyed for one hundred years.

ABOVE: Shelsley history echoes down the years as Mac Hulbert leaves the line in the perennially record-breaking ERA R4D. On this run Hulbert added to this charismatic car's laurels with a brilliant climb in 33.71sec.

ALL THE SHELSLEY BTDs

Aug 12, 1905	Ernest Instone	35hp Daimler	**77.6**
June 16, 1906	Frederick Coleman	18hp White steamer	80.6
July 13, 1907	J.E. Hutton	80hp Berliet	**67.2**
July 25, 1908	H.C. Tryon	60hp Napier	**65.4**
July 17, 1909	H.C. Holder	58hp Daimler	68.4
July 2, 1910	H.C. Holder	58hp Daimler	69.0
June 10, 1911	H.C. Holder	58hp Daimler	**63.4**
June 22, 1912	Joseph Higginson	80hp La Buire	68.8
June 7, 1913	Joseph Higginson	4.2 Vauxhall 30/98	**55.2**
July 3, 1920	Chris Bird	4.9 Sunbeam TT	58.6
Sept 10, 1921	Chris Bird	4.9 Sunbeam Indianapolis	**52.2**
July 7, 1922	Matt Park	3.0 Vauxhall TT	53.8
Sept 8, 1923	Raymond Mays	1.5 Bugatti Brescia	52.6
July 12, 1924	Cyril Paul	2.0 Beardmore	**50.5**
May 23, 1925	Henry Segrave	2.0 Sunbeam Grand Prix	53.8
July 24, 1926	Eddie Hall	4.2 Vauxhall 30/98	56.6
Sept 4, 1926	Basil Davenport	1.5 Spider	**48.8**
July 2, 1927	Basil Davenport	1.5 Spider	50.0
Sept 24, 1927	Basil Davenport	1.5 Spider	**47.8**
May 5, 1928	Basil Davenport	1.5 Spider	**46.8**
July 28, 1928	Basil Davenport	1.5 Spider	**46.2**
May 4, 1929	Basil Davenport	1.5 Spider	46.4
Sept 14, 1929	Raymond Mays	3.0 Vauxhall Villiers s/c	**45.6**
July 12, 1930	Hans Stuck	3.5 Austro-Daimler	**42.8**
Sept 13, 1930	Raymond Mays	3.0 Villiers Supercharge s/c	46.4
July 11, 1931	Dick Nash	1.5 Frazer Nash s/c	43.2
Sept 5, 1931	Raymond Mays	3.0 Villiers Supercharge s/c	46.0
June 25, 1932	Earl Howe	2.3 Bugatti Type 51 s/c	44.0
Sept 3, 1932	Dick Nash	1.5 Frazer Nash s/c	43.4
May 27, 1933	Raymond Mays	3.0 Villiers Supercharge s/c	44.8
Sept 30, 1933	Whitney Straight	2.5 Maserati 8C s/c	**41.2**

June 9, 1934	Whitney Straight	3.0 Maserati 8CM s/c	**40.0**
Sept 29, 1934	Raymond Mays	2.0 ERA R3A s/c	44.0
May 18, 1935	Raymond Mays	2.0 ERA R3A s/c	**39.6**
Sept 29, 1935	Raymond Mays	2.0 ERA R4B s/c	39.6
June 6, 1936	Raymond Mays	1.5 ERA R4B s/c	41.60
Sept 12, 1936	Raymond Mays	2.0 ERA R12B s/c	43.31
June 5, 1937	Raymond Mays	1.5 ERA R4C s/c	**39.09**
Sept 11, 1937	Fane Fane	1.5 Frazer Nash s/c	**38.77**
May 28, 1938	Raymond Mays	1.7 ERA R4D s/c	38.90
Sept 10, 1938	Raymond Mays	2.0 ERA R4D s/c	**37.86**
June 3, 1939	Raymond Mays	2.0 ERA R4D s/c	**37.37**
June 1, 1946	Raymond Mays	2.0 ERA R4D s/c	42.79
Oct 5, 1946	Ernie Lyons	0.5 Triumph motorcycle	39.44
(fastest car:	Raymond Mays	2.0 ERA R4D s/c	39.57)
June 21, 1947	Raymond Mays	2.0 ERA R4D s/c	41.50
Sept 27, 1947	Raymond Mays	2.0 ERA R4D s/c	37.69
June 12, 1948	Raymond Mays	2.0 ERA R4D s/c	37.89
Sept 25, 1948	Raymond Mays	2.0 ERA R4D s/c	37.52
June 11, 1949	Joe Fry	1.1 Freikaiserwagen s/c	**37.35**
Sept 24, 1949	George Brown	1.0 Vincent-HRD motorcycle	**37.13**
June 10, 1950	Raymond Mays	2.0 ERA R4D s/c	38.61
Sept 23, 1950	Dennis Poore	3.8 Alfa Romeo 8C-35	37.74
June 23, 1951	Ken Wharton	1.1 Cooper-JAP s/c	37.27
Sept 22, 1951	Ken Wharton	1.0 Cooper-JAP s/c	**36.62**
Aug 30, 1952	Ken Wharton	1.0 Cooper-JAP s/c	36.97
June 6, 1953	Ken Wharton	1.0 Cooper-JAP s/c	**36.60**
Aug 29, 1953	Ken Wharton	2.0 ERA R11B s/c	41.82
June 20, 1954	Ken Wharton	2.0 ERA R4D s/c	**36.58**
Aug 29, 1954	Ken Wharton	2.0 ERA R4D s/c	**35.80**
June 19, 1955	Tony Marsh	1.1 Cooper-JAP	42.60
Aug 28, 1955	Tony Marsh	1.1 Cooper-JAP s/c	36.08
June 16, 1956	Ken Wharton	2.0 ERA R4D s/c	40.91
June 30, 1956	Tony Marsh	1.1 Cooper-Climax	38.80
Aug 25, 1956	Tony Marsh	1.1 Cooper-JAP	36.02
Aug 31, 1957	Dick Henderson	1.1 Cooper-JAP s/c	35.84
June 7, 1958	Tony Marsh	1.1 Cooper-JAP s/c	37.97
June 22, 1958	Les Yarranton	2.0 Morgan Plus Four	47.70
Aug 30, 1958	Tony Marsh	1.1 Cooper-JAP s/c	**35.60**
June 14, 1959	David Boshier-Jones	1.1 Cooper-JAP s/c	36.96
June 28, 1959	George Keylock	1.5 Cooper-Climax s/c	39.40
Aug 30, 1959	David Boshier-Jones	1.1 Cooper-JAP	**35.47**
June 12, 1960	David Boshier-Jones	1.1 Cooper-JAP	35.76
June 26, 1960	David Boshier-Jones	1.1 Cooper-JAP	37.69
Aug 28, 1960	Reg Phillips	1.5 Fairley-Climax s/c	37.33
June 11, 1961	Tony Marsh	1.5 Lotus-Climax 18	35.86
July 23, 1961	George Keylock	1.5 Cooper-Climax T45 s/c	36.51
Aug 27, 1961	Tony Marsh	2.5 BRM T48/57	**34.41**
June 3, 1962	Ray Fielding	2.5 BRM T48	34.65

July 22, 1962	Ian McLaughlin	1.1 Cooper-JAP	36.04
Aug 26, 1962	George Brown	1.0 Vincent HRD motorcycle	36.82
(fastest cars:	Peter Boshier-Jones	1.1 Lotus-Climax 23	37.24
	Phil Scragg	3.8 Lister-Jaguar	37.24
June 9, 1963	Tony Marsh	2.5 BRM T48/57	**33.54**
July 21, 1963	Peter Boshier-Jones	1.2 Lotus-Climax 22 s/c	34.57
Aug 25, 1963	Peter Boshier-Jones	1.2 Lotus-Climax 22 s/c	39.16
June 14, 1964	Peter Boshier-Jones	1.2 Lotus-Climax 22 s/c	**33.35**
July 19, 1964	Peter Boshier-Jones	1.2 Lotus-Climax 22 s/c	33.99
Aug 30, 1964	Peter Boshier-Jones	1.2 Lotus-Climax 22 s/c	33.76
June 13, 1965	Tony Marsh	4.2 Marsh-GM	**32.94**
July 18, 1965	Tony Griffiths	2.5 BRM T48	34.90
Aug 29, 1965	Tony Marsh	4.2 Marsh-GM	33.50
June 12, 1966	Tony Marsh	4.2 Marsh-GM	36.22
July 24, 1966	Mike Hawley	1.6 Brabham-Ford BT16	36.92
Aug 21, 1966	Mike Hawley	1.6 Brabham-Ford BT16	40.17
June 11, 1967	Tony Marsh	4.2 Marsh-GM 4wd	**31.23**
July 23, 1967	Bryan Eccles	3.5 Brabham-GM BT18	**30.83**
Aug 20, 1967	Bryan Eccles	3.5 Brabham-GM BT18	30.98
June 9, 1968	Peter Lawson	2.1 BRM T67 4wd	31.02
July 14, 1968	Martin Brain	7.2 Cooper-Chrysler T81B	36.40
Aug 18, 1968	Peter Lawson	2.1 BRM T67 4wd	31.37
June 8, 1969	David Hepworth	4.5 Hepworth-Chevrolet 4wd	31.20
July 13, 1969	Peter Blankstone	4.5 Brabham-GM BT21B 4wd	31.26
Aug 17, 1969	Martin Brain	7.2 Cooper-Chrysler T81B	**30.72**
June 14, 1970	Nick Williamson	5.0 McLaren-Chevrolet M10A	30.72
July 11, 1970	Tony Griffiths	1.8 Brabham-FVC BT30Y	32.41
July 12, 1970	Roy Lane	2.1 TechCraft-BRM T67 4wd	30.87
Aug 16, 1970	David Hepworth	5.0 Hepworth-Chevrolet 4wd	**30.49**
June 13, 1971	David Hepworth	5.0 Hepworth-Chevrolet 4wd	**29.92**
July 10, 1971	Tony Griffiths	5.0 Brabham-Repco BT35X	31.61
July 11, 1971	Roy Lane	5.5 McLaren-Chevrolet M10B	30.30
Aug 15, 1971	David Hepworth	5.0 Hepworth-Chevrolet 4wd	**29.64**
June 11, 1972	Roy Lane	5.7 McLaren-Chevrolet M14D	31.52
July 8, 1972	Tony Griffiths	5.0 Brabham-Repco BT35X	37.36
July 9, 1972	Mike Hawley	1.6 Brabham-FVA BT35	31.10
Aug 20, 1972	Mike MacDowel	5.0 Brabham-Repco BT36X	**29.29**
June 10, 1973	Mike MacDowel	5.0 Brabham-Repco BT36X	**28.82**
July 7, 1973	Chris Cramer	2.0 March-BDA 723H	30.16
July 8, 1973	Mike MacDowel	5.0 Brabham-Repco BT36X	29.09
Aug 19, 1973	Mike MacDowel	5.0 Brabham-Repco BT36X	**28.21**
June 9, 1974	Mike MacDowel	5.0 Brabham-Repco BT36X	32.18
July 20, 1974	Ken MacMaster	1.6 GRD-BDA 272	30.48
July 21, 1974	Ken MacMaster	1.6 GRD-BDA 272	30.23
Aug 18, 1974	Mike MacDowel	5.0 Brabham-Repco BT36X	28.61
June 8, 1975	Roy Lane	5.0 McRae-Chevrolet GM1	28.74
June 28, 1975	Alister Douglas-Osborn	2.1 Pilbeam-BDG R15	28.81
June 29, 1975	Alister Douglas-Osborn	2.1 Pilbeam-BDG R15	28.67

Aug 17, 1975	Roy Lane	5.0 McRae-Chevrolet GM1	**28.03**
June 6, 1976	Alister Douglas-Osborn	3.0 Pilbeam-DFV R22	**27.92**
July 10, 1976	Alister Douglas-Osborn	3.0 Pilbeam-DFV R22	28.02
July 11, 1976	Alister Douglas-Osborn	3.0 Pilbeam-DFV R22	**27.64**
Aug 15, 1976	Alister Douglas-Osborn	3.0 Pilbeam-DFV R22	**27.39**
June 12, 1977	Martyn Griffiths	2.2 March-Hart 74B	28.71
July 9, 1977	Richard Ward	1.6 Lotus-Ford 61M	32.50
July 10, 1977	Alister Douglas-Osborn	3.0 Pilbeam-DFV R22	**27.35**
Aug 14, 1977	Alister Douglas-Osborn	3.0 Pilbeam-DFV R22	31.09
June 11, 1978	David Franklin	2.0 March-BMW 772	27.92
July 8, 1978	John Stuart	2.1 Chevron B25	31.98
July 9, 1978	Mike MacDowel	3.3 Coogar-DFV RT1	28.12
Aug 13, 1978	David Franklin	2.0 March-BMW 772	27.71
Oct 1, 1978	Peter Kaye	3.0 Pilbeam-DFV MP31	28.72
June 10, 1979	Martyn Griffiths	2.2 Pilbeam-Hart MP40	27.37
July 7, 1979	Peter Robinson	1.6 Brabham BT30	31.92
July 8, 1979	Martyn Griffiths	2.2 Pilbeam-Hart MP40	27.48
Aug 12, 1979	Martyn Griffiths	2.2 Pilbeam-Hart MP40	27.40
June 8, 1980	Alister Douglas-Osborn	3.0 Pilbeam-DFV MP31	**26.71**
July 5, 1980	Mike MacDowel	2.5 Pilbeam-Hart MP40	29.43
July 6, 1980	Martyn Griffiths	2.5 Pilbeam-Hart MP40	26.99
Aug 10, 1980	Martyn Griffiths	2.5 Pilbeam-Hart MK40	**26.60**
May 31, 1981	Alister Douglas-Osborn	3.6 Pilbeam-DFV MP47	27.30
July 4, 1981	Malcolm Dungworth	3.3 Pilbeam-DFV MP22	29.59
July 5, 1981	James Thomson	2.5 Pilbeam-Hart MP40	26.88
Aug 9, 1981	Alister Douglas-Osborn	3.6 Pilbeam-DFV MP47	**26.42**
June 6, 1982	Alister Douglas-Osborn	3.6 Pilbeam-DFV MP47	26.52
July 10, 1982	Martyn Griffiths	2.8 Pilbeam-Hart MP53	26.58
July 11, 1982	Roger Willoughby	3.5 March-Buick 712	29.48
Aug 8, 1982	Alister Douglas-Osborn	3.6 Pilbeam-DFV MP47	**26.37**
June 5, 1983	Martin Bolsover	2.8 Pilbeam-Hart MP50	26.69
July 9, 1983	Martyn Griffiths	2.8 Pilbeam-Hart MP53	27.15
July 10, 1983	John McCartney	3.0 BRM P180	33.97
Aug 14, 1983	Alister Douglas-Osborn	3.7 Pilbeam-DFY MP47	**26.08**
June 3, 1984	Alister Douglas-Osborn	4.2 Pilbeam-DFY MP55	26.88
July 7, 1984	Dave Harris	2.8 Pilbeam-Hart MP50	27.38
July 8, 1984	Roger Willoughby	3.5 March-Buick 84/RW	29.98
Aug 12, 1984	Alister Douglas-Osborn	4.2 Pilbeam-DFY MP55	26.72
June 9, 1985	Roy Lane	2.7 Pilbeam-BMW MP53	26.95
July 6, 1985	Martyn Griffiths	2.8 Pilbeam-Hart MP53	26.53
July 7, 1985	Gillian Fortescue-Thomas	4.0 Anson-Rover SA4	28.88
Aug 11, 1985	Martyn Griffiths	2.8 Pilbeam-Hart MP53	27.60
June 8, 1986	Alister Douglas-Osborn	2.8 Pilbeam-Hart MP57	26.27
July 5, 1986	Hannu Mikkola	2.1 Audi Quattro t/c	29.51
July 6, 1986	Alister Douglas-Osborn	2.8 Pilbeam-Hart MP57	26.44
Aug 10, 1986	Martyn Griffiths	2.8 Pilbeam-Hart MP53	26.54
June 7, 1987	Roy Lane	4.0 Pilbeam-DFL MP58	26.93
July 4, 1987	Peter Speakman	1.6 Brabham BT18	32.99

July 5, 1987	Martyn Griffiths	2.8 Pilbeam-Hart MP53	26.72
Aug 9, 1987	Roy Lane	4.0 Pilbeam-DFL MP58	26.14
June 5, 1988	Charles Wardle	5.0 Pilbeam-Repco MP47	26.81
July 2, 1988	Richard Brown	3.5 Martin-Rover BM24	30.43
July 3, 1988	Martyn Griffiths	2.8 Pilbeam-Hart MP53 t/c	31.95
Aug 14, 1988	Charles Wardle	5.0 Pilbeam-Repco MP47	26.24
June 4, 1989	Ray Rowan	2.8 Roman-Hart IVH	26.77
July 1, 1989	Andy Hamer	1.7 Mallock Mk 27	31.58
July 2, 1989	Roy Lane	4.0 Pilbeam-DFL MP58	26.38
Aug 13, 1989	Roy Lane	4.0 Pilbeam-DFL MP58	26.71
June 3, 1990	Martyn Griffiths	3.5 Pilbeam-DFR MP58	26.16
June 30, 1990	Bev Fawkes	4.2 Kitdeal Ultima	33.97
July 1, 1990	Martyn Griffiths	3.5 Pilbeam-DFR MP58	26.30
Aug 12, 1990	Martyn Griffiths	3.5 Pilbeam-DFR MP58	**25.86**
June 2, 1991	Martyn Griffiths	3.5 Pilbeam-DFR MP58	26.08
July 6, 1991	John Page	1.6 Reynard VW90	31.07
July 7, 1991	Roy Lane	4.0 Pilbeam-DFL MP58	26.11
Aug 11, 1991	Martyn Griffiths	3.5 Pilbeam-DFR MP58	26.03
June 7, 1992	Richard Brown	3.5 Pilbeam-DFR MP58	**25.34**
July 4, 1992	Anthony Mayman	2.0 ERA R4D s/c	34.91
July 5, 1992	Roy Lane	4.0 Pilbeam-DFL MP58	25.77
Aug 16, 1992	David Grace	3.5 Pilbeam-DFR MP58	25.96
Sept 27, 1992	David Grace	3.5 Pilbeam-DFR MP58	28.97
June 6, 1993	Mark Colton	3.5 Roman-Judd	25.96
July 3, 1993	Guy Smith	3.5 Frazer Nash	35.21
July 4, 1993	Roy Lane	4.0 Pilbeam-DFL MP58	26.60
Aug 15, 1993	David Grace	3.5 Pilbeam-DFR MP58	25.57
Sept 26, 1993	Graham Hickman	3.7 Pilbeam-DFR MP58	27.62
June 5, 1994	Mark Colton	3.5 Roman-Judd	25.91
July 2, 1994	Richard Drewett	4.7 Lotus-Ford 30	32.77
July 3, 1994	Graham Hickman	3.5 Jordan-DFR 193	29.03
Aug 14, 1994	Mark Colton	3.5 Roman-Judd	25.81
Sept 25, 1994	Roy Lane	3.5 Pilbeam-Judd MP58	34.26
June 11, 1995	Andy Priaulx	4.0 Pilbeam-DFL MP58	26.59
July 2, 1995	Roy Lane	4.0 Pilbeam-Judd MP58	26.46
July 22, 1995	Guy Smith	3.5 Frazer Nash	35.89
July 23, 1995	John Beattie	3.5 SPA-Judd HC003	28.67
Aug 13, 1995	Andy Priaulx	4.0 Pilbeam-DFL MP58	26.12
June 2, 1996	Roy Lane	4.0 Pilbeam-Judd MP58	26.31
July 6, 1996	John Venables-Lllewelyn	3.2 Alfa Romeo P3 s/c	38.26
July 7, 1995	Richard Fry	2.5 Ralt-Gould GR37	29.12
Aug 11, 1996	David Grace	3.5 Gould-Ralt-DFR GR37	26.95
Sept 22, 1996	Roy Lane	4.0 Pilbeam-Judd MP58	26.64
June 8, 1997	David Grace	3.5 Gould-Ralt-DFR GR37	26.54
July 5, 1997	Bruce Spollon	2.0 ERA R8C s/c	35.33
July 6, 1997	Richard Fry	3.5 Gould-Ralt GR37	28.18
Aug 10, 1997	David Grace	3.5 Gould-Ralt-DFR GR37	26.29
Sept 28, 1997	Roy Lane	4.0 Pilbeam-Judd MP58	26.09

May 17, 1998	Roger Moran	4.0 Pilbeam-Judd MP72	26.38
June 7, 1998	David Grace	3.5 Gould-DFR GR37	26.07
July 4, 1998	Julian Mazjub	2.3 Bugatti T35B s/c	35.64
July 5, 1998	Tom Hammonds	2.1 Audi Quattro Group B t/c	29.21
Aug 16, 1998	Roy Lane	4.0 Pilbeam-Judd MP58	26.22
May 8, 1999	Ali Serpen	3.0 MG Metro 6R4	37.13
May 9, 1999	Tom Hammonds	2.1 Audi Quattro Group B t/c	31.01
June 6, 1999	David Grace	3.5 Gould-DFR GR37	26.63
July 3, 1999	Tom Hammonds	2.1 Audi Quattro Group B t/c	29.37
July 4, 1999	Richard Drewett	5.0 Lotus-Chevrolet 70	32.49
Aug 15, 1999	Roy Lane	4.0 Pilbeam-Judd MP58	26.20
Sept 12, 1999	Roger Moran	4.0 Pilbeam-Judd MP72	26.42
June 11, 2000	David Grace	3.5 Gould-DFR GR37	26.15
July 8, 2000	Charles Dean	2.3 Bugatti T51 s/c	35.86
July 9, 2000	Chris Drewett	2.0 March 782	30.69
Aug 13, 2000	Roy Lane	4.0 Pilbeam-Judd MP58	26.05
Sept 24, 2000	Brian Moyse	1.7 Mallock Mk27SG	33.00
June 16, 2001	Graeme Wight Jr	2.5 Gould-Cosworth GR51	**25.28**
July 8, 2001	Graeme Wight Jr	2.5 Gould-Coswortrh GR51	25.49
Aug 4, 2001	Mark Budgett	1.1 Force-Suzuki SS	29.60
Aug 5, 2001	Bill Morris	2.0 Pilbeam MP82	29.21
Aug 18, 2001	Ken Sims	2.3 MG Metro 6R4 t/c	33.54
Aug 19, 2001	Graeme Wight Jr	2.5 Gould-Cosworth GR51	25.97
Sept 23, 2001	Roger Moran	4.0 Gould-Judd GR37	26.28
May 18, 2002	Deryk Young	4.0 Dellara-Judd	27.68
May 19, 2002	Deryk Young	4.0 Dellara-Judd	26.15
June 2, 2002	Graeme Wight Jr	2.5 Gould-Cosworth GR51	**24.85**
July 6, 2002	Mac Hulbert	2.0 ERA R4D s/c	34.38
July 7, 2002	Martin Baker	1.3 OMS S/F02	28.48
Aug 18, 2002	Graeme Wight Jr	2.5 Gould-Cosworth GR51	25.16
Sept 22, 2002	Deryk Young	4.0 Dellara-Judd	26.07
May 17, 2003	Tony Marsh	4.0 Gould GR37	35.55
May 18, 2003	Deryk Young	4.0 Dellara-Judd	27.49
June 8, 2003	Graeme Wight Jr	2.5 Gould-Cosworth GR51	**24.56**
July 5, 2003	Rodney Barbour	1.1 Marengo 2	28.85
July 6, 2003	Mac Hulbert	2.0 ERA R4D s/c	34.05
Aug 16, 2003	Graeme Wight Jr	2.5 Gould-Cosworth GR51	24.59
Aug 17, 2003	Adam Fleetwood	3.5 Gould-XB GR55	24.96
Sept 14, 2003	Roy Lane	4.0 Gould-Judd GR55	24.78
May 15, 2003	John Jones	2.0 Pilbeam MP82	27.60
May 16, 2004	Andy McBeath	2.0 Pilbeam MP82	28.55
June 6, 2004	Adam Fleetwood	3.5 Gould-XB GR55	**24.08**
July 3, 2004	John Jones	2.0 Pilbeam MP82	27.46
July 4, 2004	Mac Hulbert	2.0 ERA R4D s/c	33.71
Aug 15, 2004	Adam Fleetwood	3.5 Gould-XB GR55	**23.87**
Sept 12, 2004	Willem Toet	4.0 Pilbeam-Judd MP88	24.76

Shelsley Walsh records as at 1 May 2005

Outright: **Adam Fleetwood** (3.5 Gould-XB GR55), 15.8.04, 23.87sec

Pre-war car: **Mac Hulbert** (2.0 ERA R4D s/c), 4.7.04, 33.71sec

Closed car: **Tom Hammonds** (2.1 Audi Quattro Group B), 7.6.92, 28.58sec

Sports-racing car: **Nic Mann** (1.7 Mannic-Beattie t/c), 15.8.04, 26.60sec

Shelsley Special, supercharged: **Nic Mann** (1.7 Mannic-Beattie t/c), 15.8.04, 26.60sec

Shelsley Special, unsupercharged: **Mark Colton** (3.5 Roman-Judd VJ), 5.6.94, 26.26sec

Ladies: **Sue Young** (4.0 Dellara-Judd), 15.8.04, 26.98sec

Motorcycle: **Paul Jeffery** (0.5 Honda CR), 15.8.04, 31.49sec

Motorcycle and sidecar: **Jason Reeve/Steven Hoole** (1.2 FRS), 15.8.04, 31.24sec

Class records

Mod. production cars to 1400cc, road-going: **Martin Depper** (1.4 Mini-Cooper), 22.9.02, 35.15sec

Mod. production cars to 1400cc, racing: **Robert Kenrick** (1.1 Caterham Super Seven), 16.8.03, 30.80sec

Mod. production saloons 1401-2000cc: **Willem Toet** (1.9 Peugeot 205), 13.8.93, 31.02sec

Mod. production saloons over 2000cc: **Roy Standley** (2.0 Mitsubishi Lancer EVO5 t/c), 16.8.03, 31.37sec

Mod. production sports cars 1401-2000cc, roadgoing: **Trevor Willis** (2.0 Westfield SEi), 15.8.99, 32.45sec

Mod. production sports cars 1401-2000cc, racing: **Dave Kimberley** (1.0 Caterham Seven), 15.8.04, 29.41sec

Mod. production sports cars over 2000cc: **Keith Murray** (2.3 Audi Quattro t/c), 22.9.02, 28.88sec

Hillclimb Supersports: **Martin Stretton** (1.7 Vision V86), 16.8.03, 28.67sec

Sports Libre up to 2000cc: **Ian Fidoe** (2.0 Pilbeam MP43), 6.6.04, 28.16sec

Sports Libre over 2000cc: **Nic Mann** (1.7 Mannic-Beattie t/c), 15.8.04, 26.60sec

Historic 500cc Racing Cars (free fuel): **Tim Cameron** (Cooper Mk 2), 2.7.89. 34.01sec

Historic 500cc Racing Cars (pump fuel): **Steve Lawrence** (Cooper Mk 8), 17.8.03, 37.65sec

Racing cars up to 600cc: **Adam Steel** (0.6 Martlet DM8), 16.8.03, 30.19sec

Racing cars 601-1100cc: **Mark Budgett** (1.1 Force TTS), 16.8.03, 27.32sec

Racing cars 1101-1600cc: **Phil Cooke** (1.6 Force PC), 15.8.04, 26.22sec

Racing cars 1610-2000cc: **Trevor Willis** (2.9 OMS CF04), 12.9.04, 25.82sec

Racing cars over 2000cc: **Adam Fleetwood** (3.5 Gould-XB GR55), 15.8.04, 23.87sec

Classic saloons: **Simon Bridge** (2.0 Ford Anglia), 14.9.03, 35.01sec

Classic sports cars: **Rob May** (1.7 Lotus Super Seven), 2.6.02, 32.63sec

Classic sports racing and racing cars: **Peter Voigt** (3.5 TechCraft-Buick), 15.8.04, 29.25sec

Racing cars built between 1972 and 1985: **Mike Sidgwick** (2.0 Chevron B40), 15.8.04, 32.35sec

Lotus cars: **James Denty** (5.0 Lotus 70), 15.8.04, 29.09sec

PHOTOGRAPHY ACKNOWLEDGEMENTS

MAC Archive: pages 8 upper, 28 to 45, 47, 48, 49 upper, 50 to 52, 55, 56, 58 lower, 60, 61, 65 to 68, 70, 72, 75, 76, 77 lower, 78 lower, 83 to 89, 91, 94, 102 to 107, 109 upper, 114, 119, 121, 126, 134 to 137, 142, 143 upper, 144, 147 to 150, 151 upper, 156 upper, 157 to 160, 161 upper, 164 lower, 167, 170, 172 lower, 179

The McDonald Collection: pages 10, 12, 14 to 27, 71, 111, 112, 115, 132, 133, 151 lower, 155, 161 lower, 164, 165 upper, 166, 169, 172 upper, 173, 180 to 183, 186 to 189, 192 to 194, 197 to 210, 212, 213

LAT Archive: pages 8 lower, 46, 49 lower, 50, 53, 54, 58 upper, 59, 62, 63, 69, 73, 74, 77 upper, 78 upper, 79, 81, 90, 98, 99, 109 lower, 110, 146

Bob Cooper: 184
J.H. Cuff: 96, 118, 152 lower
Mike Dodman: 211
Guy Griffiths: 100, 108, 120, 122 to 125, 129, 143 lower, 153 upper
Murray Hardy: 6, 82, 92. 93, 95, 151, 152 upper
John Hayward: 195
Derek Hibbert: 11, 13, 196
Trevor Hulks: 156 lower
Bob Light: 113, 140, 162, 163, 171, 174, 176, 177, 185, 190, 191
Motor Sporting Photographers: 127, 128, 130
Paul Robinshaw: 9
Matt Spitzley: 64
Fred Taylor: 116, 131, 138, 153 lower

INDEX